The People's Bible Teachings

PREDESTINATION

Chosen In Christ

John A. Moldstad, Jr.

NORTHWESTERN PUBLISHING HOUSE
Milwaukee, Wisconsin

Second printing,   2000

Library of Congress Card 97-66994
Northwestern Publishing House
1250 N. 113th St., Milwaukee, WI 53226-3284
© 1997 by Northwestern Publishing House
Published 1997
Printed in the United States of America
ISBN 0-8100-0752-5

Table of Contents

Editor's Preface

The People's Bible Teachings is a series of books on all of the main doctrinal teachings of the Bible.

Following the pattern set by The People's Bible series, these books are written especially for laypeople. Theological terms, when used, are explained in everyday language so that people can understand them. The authors show how Christian doctrine is drawn directly from clear passages of Scripture and then how those doctrines apply to people's faith and life. Most importantly, these books show how every teaching of Scripture points to Christ, our only Savior.

The authors of The People's Bible Teachings are parish pastors and professors who have had years of experience teaching the Bible. They are men of scholarship and practical insight.

We take this opportunity to express our gratitude to Professor Leroy Dobberstein of Wisconsin Lutheran Seminary, Mequon, Wisconsin, and Professor Thomas Nass of Martin Luther College, New Ulm, Minnesota, for serving as consultants for this series. Their insights and assistance have been invaluable.

We pray that the Lord will use these volumes to help his people grow in their faith, knowledge, and understanding of his saving teachings, which he has revealed to us in the Bible. To God alone be the glory.

Curtis A. Jahn
Series Editor

Introduction

Did you know that long before you were born—yes, even before the creation of the world—God chose you as one of his believers? Does it boggle your mind to know your belief in Christ was planned by God from eternity?

God wants his dear children to know about predestination —how he has elected, chosen, them by his grace. God wants them to be comforted and encouraged as they find out more about it. "For everything that was written in the past was written to teach us, so that through endurance and the encouragement of the Scriptures we might have hope" (Romans 15:4).

This profound teaching also has much to offer for our everyday lives as followers of Christ.

- It shows us that we are saved entirely by God's grace.

- It moves us to see how Christ is the focal point of the Scriptures and all confessional Lutheran theology.

- It assures us we don't need to be afraid as we face the future, because the God who controls the present and the past controls the future as well.

- It affects our strategy for doing mission work.

- Finally, it affirms that God has chosen us to be different—to be holy and blameless in his sight.

Predestination is a deep teaching. It is not the "milk" given to novices and new converts. It is solid food (1 Corinthians 3:2). Even mature Christians will have some questions on predestination.

Unfortunately, while trying to explain predestination, some have stumbled. Problems usually arise in this and similar areas of theology when people attempt to use human reason as a litmus test for the truths of God's Word. Our sinful minds often try to force a union between God's teachings and our own reason when it cannot be done.

In this respect we can learn a lesson from Dr. Martin Luther. He was a master at dealing with the Word. He never put God's truth to any kind of human litmus test. Luther put reason in its proper perspective when he said:

> God has given men reason so that they can milk cows, bridle horses, and know that a hundred gulden are more than ten. Show your wisdom there; be a master and a good helper; use your knowledge. But here, when it comes to the question how we are to be saved, in heavenly matters and matters of faith, stop your reason, keep still, listen and say: Here I can no longer operate; this is different from the matters related above. Curb your reason, therefore, and say: I do not understand this; I will not figure or measure it but will keep still and listen, for it is beyond my measuring and is incomprehensible to reason.[1]

With that said, may the Lord bless our study of predestination. With the psalmist we pray, "Let me understand the teaching of your precepts; then I will meditate on your wonders" (Psalm 119:27).

1

Laying the Background

Before we look specifically at what the Bible teaches about predestination, let's review nine basic scriptural truths about God's gracious plan of salvation for sinners. This review will help us better understand the place God wants this Bible teaching to have in our Christian faith and lives.

1. All people are sinners and so spiritually depraved by nature that all would perish eternally without divine help.

> Everyone has turned away, they have together become corrupt; there is no one who does good, not even one. (Psalm 53:3)

> The sinful mind is hostile to God. (Romans 8:7)

> The result of one trespass was condemnation for all men. (Romans 5:18)

> Surely I was sinful at birth, sinful from the time my mother conceived me. (Psalm 51:5)

What is our view of humanity? How do we see ourselves in light of our sinfulness? Do we see the spiritual sinkhole into which our souls have plummeted? Could it be that the hole appears less deep than it really is?

The expression "There's a little good in everyone" often is not recognized for what it actually implies: The bad that dwells in people by nature is perhaps not that bad after all! Yet Romans 5:18 informs us that the sinkhole into which we all have fallen is truly a bottomless pit! Such a pit cannot be scaled by any human efforts. The trespass of Adam (original sin) so permeates all of us who have come from his family tree that even from the time of our conception and birth, we carry the stamp "condemned." This is a key concept for us to grasp. Otherwise, God's remarkable way of pulling us from hell's pit will carry little, if any, meaning for our lives.

2. God wants all people to be saved.

> [God] wants all men to be saved and to come to a knowledge of the truth. (1 Timothy 2:4)

> He is patient with you, not wanting anyone to perish, but everyone to come to repentance. (2 Peter 3:9)

We often think, "Oh, if only I knew what God really wanted!" Maybe we don't know specifically why he lets certain things happen to us. Maybe we don't know precisely what occupations he wants us to pursue or exactly where he wants us to live. But make no mistake: we can be sure of what he wants most of all. God wants us and every other person to share in his free salvation! Peter says this is the very reason God allows the world to continue without destroying it. More people are being added to his kingdom, just as he graciously desires!

3. God already has redeemed the entire world through the work of his Son, Jesus Christ.

No further payment for our sins, nor for the sins of anyone, is needed. Why? If the holy blood of the Son of God has redeemed us from our sins, we truly have been set free from any condemnation for them!

> God was reconciling the world to himself in Christ, not counting men's sins against them. (2 Corinthians 5:19)

> He is the atoning sacrifice for our sins, and not only for ours but also for the sins of the whole world. (1 John 2:2)

> For God so loved the world that he gave his one and only Son, that whoever believes in him shall not perish but have eternal life. (John 3:16)

This is the way God reached into the bottomless pit. He placed his Son right where you and I were held hostage by sin and Satan. We were in the middle of a spiritual, eternal free fall. Jesus came with flesh and blood and took our place inside that ugly pit—he didn't just come to meet us at the rim. He died the death we deserved. The ransom payment was no bank full of greenbacks subject to devaluation and inflation, but the lifeblood of God himself— pure, undefiled, and priceless! And because of this blood's amazing power, not a single soul is exempt from the blessing it imparts.

4. God calls or invites all people to faith with equal earnestness.

Besides God's desire to save all and his act of redeeming all, the Holy Spirit—the giver and preserver of spiritual life—sincerely concentrates on calling all people to faith in Christ.

> "As surely as I live, declares the Sovereign LORD, I take no pleasure in the death of the wicked, but rather that they turn from their ways and live." (Ezekiel 33:11)

> For God has bound all men over to disobedience so that he may have mercy on them all. (Romans 11:32)

"Maybe God tries a little harder to catch some with the gospel than he does others." This erroneous thought may enter our minds from time to time when we look around and see even members of the same family divided in their attitudes toward Christ. But consider this: Even in the invitational call to faith, we see from the Bible itself that God is equally serious about rescuing every lost and condemned sinner. He takes no pleasure in observing anyone perish.

5. God alone works faith in a person's heart and keeps that saving faith alive.

> No one can say, "Jesus is Lord," except by the Holy Spirit. (1 Corinthians 12:3)

> For it is God who works in you to will and to act according to his good purpose. (Philippians 2:13)

"I believe . . ." With these words we begin the Apostles' Creed. Behind the words, behind the confessor, behind the faith in the heart, God himself is at work. No other explanation will do. Either the act of faith is all *God's* doing, *God's* miracle, or else it is a sham. The Holy Spirit, aided by no one or nothing else, moves us to acclaim Christ as our Savior.

6. The entire credit for a sinner's conversion and final salvation belongs only to God.

Scripture completely rules out the possibility of letting this credit, even in the smallest amount, go to humans themselves or any other cause.

> For it is by grace you have been saved, through faith—and this not from yourselves, it is the gift of God—not by works, so that no one can boast. (Ephesians 2:8,9)

> It does not, therefore, depend on man's desire or effort, but on God's mercy. (Romans 9:16)

> When the kindness and love of God our Savior appeared, he saved us, not because of righteous things we had done, but because of his mercy. He saved us through the washing of rebirth and renewal by the Holy Spirit. (Titus 3:4,5)

The apostle Paul leaves no room for defining God's grace as less than a *gift* from a gracious benefactor to a poor helpless beggar. Believing brings no boast in self because human qualities, works, and achievements play no part in *why* and *how* God saves. From start to finish, the boast is "Christ!" Faith is God's gift. When a gift is placed into a hand, would a person dare say, "But I did *my* part by taking it?" That is foreign thinking to the receiver of salvation by faith!

7. Rejection of Christ in unbelief and the resulting consequence of eternal damnation is the individual person's responsibility. God can never be blamed for even one sinner being lost.

What if some did not have faith? Will their lack of faith nullify God's faithfulness? Not at all! Let God be true, and every man a liar. (Romans 3:3,4)

"O Jerusalem, Jerusalem, you who kill the prophets and stone those sent to you, how often I have longed to gather your children together, as a hen gathers her chicks under her wings, but you were not willing." (Matthew 23:37)

"You always resist the Holy Spirit!" (Acts 7:51)

As firmly as Scripture stresses that all glory goes to God for saving people, so firmly does it also stress that unbelievers dig their own eternal graves. "But how can that be? If God alone does the saving, isn't he to be faulted for any who are lost?" Admittedly, this truth seems illogical. Yet God must be God. His grace must always be grace, and rejection really is a fault of the sinner stemming from what our first parents did at the tree in the Garden of Eden.

8. God uses the means of grace alone to bring people to faith. Baptism and hearing the Word convey forgiveness of sins to the heart. The Lord's Supper also brings Christ's forgiveness in order to strengthen faith.

Consequently, faith comes from hearing the message, and the message is heard through the word of Christ. (Romans 10:17)

"No one can enter the kingdom of God unless he is born of water and the Spirit." (John 3:5)

The word of God . . . is at work in you who believe. (1 Thessalonians 2:13)

"Tunnel of love" is a worldly expression for sensual love. We could say that *"funnel* of love" depicts the means through which God channels his divine love to us. He doesn't filter it through any screen tests. He doesn't have to. It's pure and it's for all. From the cross of his Son, God pipes his pardon to us through Baptism and the Word. Through these means the Spirit does his work. Faith itself, says Paul, results only from "hearing the message" (Romans 10:17).

9. *The will of God revealed in his Word must always take precedence over human reason and logic, even when what the Word clearly says and what logic clearly teaches are at odds with each other.*

Explanations beyond our comprehension are found in the infinite wisdom of the Creator. Our assignment this side of heaven is to stay strictly with what he has set forth in the Scriptures.

> The spiritual man makes judgments about all things, but he himself is not subject to any man's judgment: "For who has known the mind of the Lord that he may instruct him?" But we have the mind of Christ. (1 Corinthians 2:15,16)

> "Ah, Sovereign LORD, you have made the heavens and the earth by your great power and outstretched arm. Nothing is too hard for you." (Jeremiah 32:17)

> Oh, the depth of the riches of the wisdom and knowledge of God! How unsearchable his judgments, and his paths beyond tracing out! (Romans 11:33)

Only by keeping these basic truths of Scripture clearly before us will we be able to understand correctly and appreciate fully what Scripture teaches about predestination. By first reviewing these basic truths of God's plan of salvation, we are following the example the apostle Paul

set down in his letter to the Romans. Paul does not begin
Romans with predestination. Instead, he spends most of
the first eight chapters thoroughly teaching the basic
truths of salvation, which we have summarized in this
chapter. Only at the end of Romans 8 does Paul first present predestination and demonstrate how Christians are to
properly apply this teaching to their lives.

In the following chapters we will take a close look at the
Scripture passages that teach predestination, or election.

2

Our Election

Now that we have reviewed the basic scriptural teachings about God's plan of salvation, we will begin our study of the Scripture passages that speak about election. Romans 8 and 9 and Ephesians 1 present the doctrine in detail. In this chapter we will take a close look at a portion of Romans 8. Before we proceed, we offer this basic operating definition of *election*:

> The truth that God from eternity has in his mercy chosen people to everlasting life through faith in Jesus Christ and that this faith is worked in them by means of God's Word and sacraments.

Romans 8:28-30—background
"We know that in all things God works for the good of those who love him, who have been called according to

his purpose. For those God foreknew he also predestined to be conformed to the likeness of his Son, that he might be the firstborn among many brothers. And those he predestined, he also called; those he called, he also justified; those he justified, he also glorified" (Romans 8:28-30).

What is God saying to us in these verses? We cannot overlook their background. We need to see how the apostle Paul lays the groundwork for his presentation on election. We don't want to miss the beautiful way election fits into God's entire plan of salvation for us!

The letter to the Romans unquestionably is the most thorough doctrinal letter from the hand of Paul, and it follows a definite pattern. The first five chapters address the question of how a sinner is declared forgiven and holy in the eyes of God. Paul gives the theme of the whole letter in 1:17, "The righteous will live by faith."

Do *all* people have the same opportunity for salvation? Might Jews have an edge on Gentiles? Could it be that works—good deeds done by those who are faithful (such as Abraham)—count in some way toward their justification (that is, the declaration by the holy judge that sinners are just, righteous, not guilty, forgiven)? Paul answers these questions thoroughly and emphatically.

In Romans 1–5 alone at least 18 distinct passages explicitly state that sinners receive God's verdict of justified, or forgiven, only through faith in Christ. And faith in Christ is contrasted with salvation by works. For example, Paul writes, "[All] are justified freely by his grace through the redemption that came by Christ Jesus" (3:24), and then he also says, "David . . . speaks of the blessedness of the man to whom God credits righteousness apart from works" (4:6).

Romans 6 and 7 address the natural concern believers have once they know they have been declared forgiven purely by the life, death, and resurrection of Christ: *How shall I now live?* Paul opens the discussion with a preposterous thought: "What shall we say, then? Shall we go on sinning so that grace may increase? By no means!" (6:1,2). The very opposite of living in sin is on the minds of believers because of their burning desire to *thank* Christ!

Moving through the seventh chapter into the eighth, we note something interesting. After discussing the daily fight against sin, Paul acknowledges that doubts will occur. Why doubts? We don't always carry out the lives we *want* to live in thankfulness to Christ. In fact, an honest evaluation of our own lives would lead us to despair. We sin again and again. If *Paul* called himself a "wretched man" (7:24) as he reflected on the way sin continued to worm its way into his life as a Christian, would *we* say any less of ourselves? Knowing this temptation to despair, the apostle takes us right back to the only place we have refuge. He again powerfully presents the gospel, reminding us "there is now no condemnation for those who are in Christ Jesus" (8:1). This spurs us on to live new lives, focusing our minds on "what the Spirit desires" (verse 5).

Now Paul follows with this thought: Since the Holy Spirit has brought us to faith in Christ, making us "heirs of God and co-heirs with Christ" (verse 17) of life everlasting, why should we worry? Even when we suffer bodily pain and mental or emotional affliction, these things can't compare "with the glory that will be revealed in us" (verse 18). We eagerly await the great day of final deliverance, the day of spectacular glory!

We are now prepared for the way Paul presents election. He speaks to *those who already understand* that their sins have been forgiven and that through the Holy Spirit they

have been made children of God. Any scriptural instruct-
ing on election begins on this premise.

In an excellent sermon on election, Dr. Siegbert Becker
drew attention to this point:

> This we must know [that Christ is our Savior and that our
> sins are forgiven] before we can profitably discuss the doc-
> trine of election. When Luther was a monk in the
> monastery, he was greatly troubled by the doctrine of elec-
> tion, and he worried about it day and night. One day he
> told Dr. Staupitz, who was vicar general of the Augus-
> tinian order of monks to which Luther belonged, about his
> fears. Dr. Staupitz told him, "Brother Martin, first find
> yourself in the wounds of Christ, and then you can be sure
> of your election." Luther never forgot this advice, and he
> speaks of it again and again in his writings. He says that if
> it had not been for Dr. Staupitz, he would have despaired.
> And this advice of Dr. Staupitz is still good advice today.[2]

Romans 8:28-30—explanation

Returning to Romans 8, we notice that Paul broaches
the subject of election in the immediate context of a
promise to believers. The promise is that "all things"—
even the hard-to-fathom things—are worked out by God
"for the good of those who love him" (verse 28). To show
that "those who love [God]" are none other than the very
ones whom God himself has brought to faith, Paul adds,
"who have been called according to his purpose."

The reason believers are not to worry in spite of afflic-
tions and weakness is because they have been called to be
God's own. Paul strengthens this by adding, "For those God
foreknew" (verse 29). The prefix "fore" in "foreknew" dates
God's knowledge back to eternity. The thought here is:
"Don't you know that God from eternity has embraced you
as his dear children? Prior to your birth, totally apart from

any moment in time when you could plead your case before him, God already put his claim on you!" Israel did not *do* anything to be a favored nation but was set apart by God to be a nation through which other nations would be blessed. So also we did not *do* anything to be foreknown by God, but in love he has set us apart for his very own family.

God the Father's will and intention was that after this life we should share with him the perfect bliss of heaven. He had a clear-cut plan on how this would happen for us. The specifics of that plan were formed in eternity!

There's more. Paul says God also "predestined [us] to be conformed to the likeness of his Son" (verse 29). God not only foresaw how people would come into his kingdom, he actually preselected, or preappointed in a determined way, those who would have eternal life through faith in his Son.

The original Greek word for "predestine" gives us a vivid and wonderful picture. It envisions the erecting of a fence or boundary around one's property. The erecting of this security line is not done in any haphazard way, but with determination. So when we speak of God predestining us for life in heaven, we might think of it as his way of putting a fence around us. He has made us his own property! That, of course, means "hands off" to sin, death, and the devil, our adversaries who also desire to have us as their own.

We, like all people, have deserved eternal death in hell because of our sinfulness. Although God created us, our rebelling against him removed us from his property. We landed ourselves on the other side of the fence. So much did sin wreck the scene! But God had determined beforehand to put his protective fence around us. This only could happen in one way: by having us "be conformed to the likeness of his Son" (verse 29). Paul here calls the Son of God "the firstborn among many brothers." Jesus became our brother. The eternal Son of God took into his person our human nature (flesh and blood and soul) in order to make the necessary substitutionary sacrifice for the sins of all. Through faith in what Christ, our flesh-and-blood brother, did, we are given new birth! This spiritual birth assures us we will reign with Christ eternally in heaven. This is how God planned ahead of time for us to be his own. He predestined, or elected, us to be his very own children through faith in his Son.

But we may be troubled by the question "How can I know if I'm among the elect?" None of us was able to sit in on the counsel of God prior to creation. Yet Paul does give us an answer: "Those he predestined, he also called; those he called, he also justified; those he justified, he also glorified" (verse 30). The apostle wants us to see the close connection between God's election from eternity and our call to faith at the present time.

Aren't you, at this very moment in your life, hearing and believing the gospel? If so—that is, if we surely are among the ones God has called to faith in Christ—then why ever doubt we are also among the elect, the chosen? As Professor J. P. Meyer once put it: "Wherever the call is heard, there we have the instrument with which God implemented His predestination. Whom He predestined, them He also called."[3]

When God called you to faith, he presented you with your justification. "Those he called, he also justified" (verse 30). By not sparing his own Son but letting him suffer on the cross, God has proclaimed you and me and all people forgiven and free of the guilt and punishment for sin. This is justification. In verse 30 Paul clearly speaks of receiving that justification *by faith*. In other words, he is speaking here of people who have received by faith God's verdict of "justified," "forgiven," for he quickly adds, "those he justified, he also glorified." In due time God will take all his believers to heavenly bliss. But don't forget: Our glory is also a fact *now* by faith in the Lord of glory, who has bought us with his blood!

Let's review what we have learned about election from Paul's words in Romans 8:

- We are Christians not of our own doing but because God wanted us to be Christians. The gift concept prevails!

- God foreknew us from eternity as his dear children. He is the giver here; we are the receivers.

- From eternity God deliberately chose us to be his own through faith in his Son.

- In time God called us to faith in Christ, through whom we receive forgiveness of sins and justification. By this faith we possess eternal glory.

Later in our study we will look at other verses in Romans 8, as well as in Romans 9. In the next chapter, we proceed with the words of Paul in Ephesians 1.

3

Our Election Is *in Christ*

The whole Bible is centered in Christ. Whether we are reading in the Old Testament or perusing the New Testament, Christ leaps out as the intended focus. In a similar way, election is completely centered in Christ. He is the whole basis for our election. No biblical section on election drives home this point as forcefully as Ephesians 1. The red thread of *in Christ* runs throughout Paul's entire doxology, with the phrase (or one like it) occurring 12 times in verses 3-12. We give special attention now to verses 4-6.

Ephesians 1:4-6
Writing to the Christians in Ephesus, the apostle Paul comforted his hearers with these words: "For he chose us

25

in him before the creation of the world to be holy and
blameless in his sight. In love he predestined us to be
adopted as his sons through Jesus Christ, in accordance
with his pleasure and will—to the praise of his glorious
grace, which he has freely given us in the One he loves"
(1:4-6).

To explain the key points of this section, we will focus
on certain phrases from the pen of the apostle.

"Chose us in him"

The verb Paul uses, translated in the NIV as "chose," is
best rendered "elected." It is different from the verb he
uses for "predestined" (in verses 5 and 11), yet the meaning is similar: picking out some from a large number. "For
many are invited, but few are chosen" (Matthew 22:14).
We are talking about individual people, not abstract quo-
tas! In electing us out of the world's enormous population,
God didn't conduct some kind of imaginary audition,
where multitudes from all cultures and races paraded
before him, displaying what they could offer. God had
only one basis for electing us from the massive population
to be his own: "in him," that is *in Christ!* Christ is the cornerstone of God's whole plan of salvation. There is no salvation apart from him. By the same token, in Christ is
every part and every benefit of salvation.

People often are chosen to receive honors and awards
and to enjoy the limelight of public attention. The choosing in these cases is due to some accomplishments or some
qualities exhibited by those chosen for acknowledgment.
How different it is with God's choosing individual people
to enjoy life eternal with him! No human achievements,
no human traits, no human qualities of any kind played a
part in God's election. How could it? Sin can only bring

death. Saturated with sinfulness, even from conception and birth, we were by nature objects of God's wrath, deserving eternal death. But God *has* chosen us, nevertheless! He has redeemed us! He has adopted us as his dear children! The motive and reason for our election is all wrapped up in the merits of his own Son. This alone explains why the Lord says, "I have loved you with an everlasting love" (Jeremiah 31:3).

The fact that our election is in Christ means it is based on and carried out fully *by God's grace*, his undeserved love. "So too, at the present time there is a remnant chosen by grace" (Romans 11:5). Again, we read, "[God] has saved us and called us to a holy life—not because of anything we have done but because of his own purpose and grace" (2 Timothy 1:9).

"Before the creation of the world"

Here too we see why our election must be entirely in Christ. From eternity, before the universe was formed and there was not even a single angel to give him praise, God thought about us. He saw the future and our predicament of being trapped in sin and unbelief. He then planned to save us and give us life. To such a degree did he plan this, that God even chose the redeeming sacrifice of his Son before any of his acts in creating the world. "He [Christ] was chosen before the creation of the world, but was revealed in these last times for your sake" (1 Peter 1:20). The only way our election could come about is because Christ Jesus is "the Lamb that was slain from the creation of the world" (Revelation 13:8).

The apostle Paul also expressed our election from eternity in his second letter to Timothy: "This grace was given us in Christ Jesus before the beginning of time" (1:9). In the Lutheran Confessions, our Lutheran fathers stressed this "eternity" factor as a source of great comfort:

> God was so deeply concerned about every individual Christian's conversion, righteousness, and salvation and so faithfully minded about it that "even before the foundation of the world was laid" he held counsel and ordained "according to his purpose" how he would bring me thereto and keep me therein.[4]

The Lutheran hymn writer Paul Gerhardt has captured the awe of our election from eternity in his hymn "I Stand Beside Thy Manger Here":

> Thy love, O Lord, before my birth
> Thou didst elect to show me,
> And for my sake didst come to earth
> Before I e'er did know Thee.
> Yea, long before Thy gracious hand
> Created me, Thy grace had planned
> To make Thee mine forever.
> (*Evangelical Lutheran Hymnary* 129:2)

"To be holy and blameless in his sight"

Is this referring to our lives of good works following faith? No, our lives of good works are never the *basis* of God's election, but the *result*. Here Paul's emphasis is on what *God* has done for us in Christ. The major goal of our election is to have us appear before God, not only on judgment day but right now, holy and completely faultless. Because of Christ's atoning death we have such holiness! In Ephesians 1:7 Paul stresses, "In him we have redemption through his blood, the forgiveness of sins." No wonder, as Isaiah had said, God "remembers your sins no more" (43:25)! Christ's death, the death of the Holy One in whom God's fullness dwells, has truly made us "holy in

his sight, without blemish and free from accusation"
(Colossians 1:22). We have had this holiness from our
Savior pronounced upon us in the gospel and in our bap-
tisms, and by faith we grab it for our very own.

Since we are "blameless in his sight" purely through
faith in Christ, we eagerly desire to live blamelessly in
accordance with God's holy commandments. We are chosen to be different. Why should we live like the world
when we are members of a better world? We want to live
in thankfulness to him who died for us. An important purpose for Christ's work in our lives is "to purify for himself a
people that are his very own, eager to do what is good"
(Titus 2:14). "For we are God's workmanship, created in
Christ Jesus to do good works, which God prepared in
advance for us to do" (Ephesians 2:10).

*"In love he predestined us to be adopted as his sons through
Jesus Christ, in accordance with his pleasure and will"*

Say it with emphasis: "In love!" Endless volumes could
be written about God's love, and one volume has, the
Holy Bible. In the New Testament the Greek word *agape*
is used for God's love for us. This word implies a love that
does what is necessary to help others even if they don't
deserve it. It is a giving love, a sharing love. Human illus-
trations of sacrificial love, such as a mother dying as she
shields her child from certain death or a battalion com-
mander falling on a grenade for his troops, cannot ade-
quately depict the great *agape* love of God for us. As
touching as those examples are, how can they fully portray
the immense love of the Creator willing to sacrifice his
own Son so that we enemy creatures could survive and—
more than that—live endlessly to the full?

For this goal to be accomplished, God "predestined us to be adopted as his sons" (Ephesians 1:5). In football every coach loves a player who is not distracted from moving the ball down the gridiron and over the goal line. Wouldn't it be something if a coach could predestine a player to receive the goal? In a far more important "playing field," our God has predestined us to receive the highest goal of all. By having us use his Word and sacraments, he keeps us moving forward within the boundary limits. Through faith in Christ we head straight for the goal.

How does God do this? Predestination occurs by adoption. Payments and paper signing play an important part in adoption. A guarantee must be given that unnatural children will have the full rights accorded natural children. Jesus has done all this for you and me! The payment of his lifeblood is the indelible ink guaranteeing our adoption into God's family. No legal technicality could be posed as an obstacle to our receiving "children of God" status, even though we had been children of the devil. God's good pleasure ensured we were personal recipients of his grace. Baptism is the sacred rite by which God inducted our names into his family. "You are all sons of God through faith in Christ Jesus, for all of you who were baptized into Christ have clothed yourselves with Christ" (Galatians 3:26,27). Again, the point is driven home: Our election is *in Christ!*

"To the praise of his glorious grace, which he has freely given us in the One he loves"

Is this *our* praising God? In his commentary on Ephesians, Professor Irwin Habeck replies:

> Some restrict this praise to our act of praising him. . . . But comparing this verse with 1:12 and 14; 2:7; 3:10 and 2 Thessalonians 1:11, I conclude that we also are to his praise just by what we are. When we see our fellow believers and they see us, we are amazed at what God's grace is able to do. Thus we are to his praise. . . . This effect of calling forth admiration and amazement will continue through the judgment into the consummation in glory.[5]

The gift of our election is in connection with the beloved Son of God. Ephesians 1:11 reminds us of the same: "In him we were also chosen." If the beloved one from eternity, the one chosen by God to be the Savior, is the very one on whom our election hinges, how can we fail? Jesus received the highest accolade: "This is my Son, whom I love; with him I am well pleased" (Matthew 3:17).

Let's review how Paul in Ephesians ties up our election *in Christ:*

- Before the world was created, God picked us out of the world's population to be followers of Jesus Christ.

- Holiness is needed for heaven. So God arranged through Christ to have us be "blameless in his sight." We are called to be his new creation in Christ.

- In love he adopted us as his children through Holy Baptism.

- By connecting us to God's beloved one, our election praises his undeserved love, freely given to us.

Where does Paul have us look to determine if we are among the elect? He directs us to the one in whom alone is forgiveness of sins: Jesus Christ. "In him we have redemption through his blood, the forgiveness of sins" (1:7). We see what Christ has done for us on the cross in taking away the guilt of our sin. We believe and know we are forgiven for his sake. We are headed for eternal life. There can be no doubt about our election when we are holding on to Christ by faith.

What in Christ *does not mean*

Since election is tied to Christ, it is impossible for any person to be chosen for heaven without ever coming to faith. The Bible clearly teaches that people who in their time of grace do not come to faith in Christ cannot be regarded as part of the elect. "All who were appointed for eternal life believed" (Acts 13:48). There is no room in election for supposing that even if people never had the chance to hear the gospel and believe it, this would have no ill effect on them spiritually or eternally as long as "election tipped in their favor." Unbelief always condemns. God's election of people *in Christ* means that only through faith in Christ can a person be counted among the chosen.

We also know that the elect cannot include any who believe but then fall away prior to death. *In Christ* means everlasting life (which only the elect enjoy) comes to those who are believers at the time of their departure from this earth.

Election's relationship to faith

"Am I saved by election, or am I saved by faith?" is an important question to answer. God's election should not be perceived as arbitrary, eliminating faith as the way for his elect to be brought into the kingdom of heaven. Faith can never be overlooked or disregarded in God's decree of election. Consider this pertinent passage from 2 Thessalonians: "God chose you to be saved through the sanctifying work of the Spirit and through belief in the truth" (2:13). Belief in the truth is a necessary component of God's election. God brings those he has chosen to faith in the Savior by the preaching of his gospel. The Bible's definition of election therefore does not and cannot eliminate either the absolute necessity of Christ's work of redemption nor the matter of faith ("the sanctifying work of the Spirit"). Each of these doctrines is to receive its proper emphasis. So to say, "I am saved by election," is surely no less than to say, "I am saved by faith."

Who are the elect? Only God knows the full number. Through faith in Christ he wants us to know for certain that *we* are in that number. In light of what we have learned, we can say this: The elect are all those who believe in Jesus Christ at the moment of death and thus are taken to heaven. Election is always through faith *in Christ*.

4

Our Election Is through the Holy Spirit and the Means of Grace

Before a contractor begins to build a house, he conceives a plan in his mind. How will he build? What materials will he use? Observers at the building site may not have any prior knowledge of how the plan developed in the mind of the contractor. Yet they begin to see the plan unfold as the blueprint is shown and the project gets underway. It is safe to conclude that the contractor will keep building by his plan until his original purpose is fulfilled.

God has informed us of his plan to build a house, a spiritual house. This house is the Christian church, the elect of God from around the world. The writer of Hebrews says: "Christ is faithful as a son over God's house. And we are his house" (3:6). God has a definite plan for building this house. Like the observers at the building site, we were not there at the moment in eternity when God drew up his plans for the house. But we can and do know from observing the blueprint of God's Word and the growth in God's kingdom how the plan works.

The plan

What is God's plan for building his house, that is, for causing sinners such as you and me to be numbered among his elect, destined for the eternal kingdom of glory? His blueprint for building his kingdom includes two key components: the means of grace and the Holy Spirit working through those means.

The means of grace

The means by which God works faith in people's hearts and keeps that faith alive are called the means of grace. These means are the Word of the gospel, which is called "the power of God for the salvation of everyone who believes" (Romans 1:16); Baptism, described as "the washing of rebirth and renewal by the Holy Spirit" (Titus 3:5); and the Lord's Supper, in which the true body and blood of Christ are offered to the communicants (Luke 22:19,20). Actually, one word can sum up all these means of grace: gospel. In these means the entire good news of Christ's forgiveness of sins for the world is brought to the hearts of individual people. Since these means are the only way set forth in Holy Scripture for a sinner to come to faith in Jesus, they are indispensable tools for building God's house. As much as a carpenter depends on his hammer and nails and his saw and boards in order to begin and complete his work of building an earthly house, so much—and far more—does God depend on his means of grace to erect his kingdom.

Why should this be? Doesn't God, unlike an earthly builder, have all power at his possession at any time? Even though a carpenter has to use a tool that he himself has not crafted, can't God do without any tools to build his kingdom of the elect? Yes, God certainly can. Who dares to limit the one of whom Job remarked, "I know that you can do all things; no plan of yours can be thwarted" (Job 42:2)? But Job's comment reminds us to keep two things straight: (1) God certainly can do all things without any use of means, if he chooses to do so, but (2) when he has made a plan by his own authority and will, no one dare criticize it! The plan of using the Word and the sacraments to give his elect people heaven through Christ is the irrevocable blueprint from the infallible world designer himself!

As we have hinted, this plan often is maligned. Many, for example, think the use of preaching and Baptism is too simplistic and unassuming to be the way God chooses to bring people to faith and give them eternal life. Just as Naaman the Syrian scoffed at the prophet Elisha's insistence that he wash himself in the Jordan River to be rid of his leprosy, so also in our day people sometimes scoff at the water of Baptism. The cry from Naaman, "Are not . . . the rivers of Damascus . . . better than any of the waters of Israel?" (2 Kings 5:12), finds parallel thought in the expression "How can water do such great things?" But the apostle Paul has the answer for all who attack God's design, his method, for building his kingdom. Paul reminds us that the message of the cross of Christ, which the world sees as *minus* saving potential, is God's own *plus* sign for a needy world. "For the message of the cross is foolishness to those who are perishing, but to us who are being saved it is the power of God. For since in the wisdom of God the world through its wisdom did not know him, God was pleased through the foolishness of what was preached to save those who believe" (1 Corinthians 1:18,21).

The Holy Spirit's work is necessary

Apart from the work the Holy Spirit does in converting and in preserving faith, it is impossible to carry out God's eternal election of souls. The builder himself must construct this special house. In his explanation to the Third Article of the Apostles' Creed, Martin Luther expressed the need for the Holy Spirit: "I believe that I cannot by my own thinking and choosing believe in Jesus Christ, my Lord, or come to him. But the Holy Spirit has called me by the gospel, enlightened me with his gifts, sanctified and kept me in the true faith."

These familiar words of Luther are precisely what Scripture teaches. Jesus once said to the Jews who did not believe in him, "No one can come to me unless the Father who sent me draws him" (John 6:44). The heavenly Father has arranged for the third person of the Trinity to do the work of drawing sinners to himself, for "no one can say, 'Jesus is Lord,' except by the Holy Spirit" (1 Corinthians 12:3).

Our election is tied to the work of the Holy Spirit. In 2 Thessalonians 2:13 we are told, "God chose you to be saved through the sanctifying work of the Spirit." Here the word *sanctifying* is used in a broad sense to include all that the Holy Spirit does in turning our hearts to God and keeping us in the faith until everlasting life. Literally the wording is "in [or by] sanctification of the Spirit." The emphasis is on an activity that is entirely God's doing.

This activity, the working of faith, is attributed to the Holy Spirit and is essential to our election for heaven.

Why is the Holy Spirit needed to work faith? Don't human beings make decisions about many things in life? Can't we decide, for example, how to raise our families, where to live, and where to work? If we decide important matters like these, how can anyone say for sure that only God can create and preserve faith? In an excellent article on free will, the writers of the Formula of Concord have given the appropriate answer:

> Thus Scripture denies to the intellect, heart, and will of the natural man every capacity, aptitude, skill, and ability to think anything good or right in spiritual matters, to understand them, to will them, to undertake them, to begin them, to do them, to accomplish or to cooperate in them as of himself. . . . "The unspiritual man does not receive (or, as the Greek word actually has it, does not grasp, take hold of, or apprehend) the gifts of the Spirit of God (that is, he has no capacity for spiritual things) for they are folly to him, and he is not able to understand them" (I Cor. 2:14). Much less will he be able truly to believe the Gospel, give his assent to it, and accept it as truth. For the mind that is set on the flesh (the natural man's understanding) "is hostile to God; it does not submit to God's law, indeed it cannot" (Rom. 8:7).[6]

So thoroughly are we sinners enslaved by the effects upon our souls of the first sin of Adam and Eve, we would not even nibble at the gospel for a taste if the Holy Spirit did not activate our taste buds. Picture a helpless soul groping in utter darkness until someone flicks on a floodlight. A hymn writer portrayed the Holy Spirit breaking through our dark night "with the beams of truth unclouded," and so we sing, "You alone to God can win us; you must work all good within us" (*Christian Worship* [CW] 221:2). Dr. Luther penned similar words in his Large Catechism: "Neither you nor I could ever know anything of Christ, or believe in him and take him as our Lord, unless these were first offered to us and bestowed on our hearts through the preaching of the Gospel by the Holy Spirit."[7]

Faith: God's action in us

Election does not involve a haphazard system resembling the way lottery balls roll out of a rotating transparent cylinder. From the Bible we have no reason to think the Holy Spirit will simply zap a person out of the blue, using no means of contact, and settle the individual inside the fenced area encircling the chosen of God. We are saved only through faith, which itself is God's own work in us. But our faith needs to latch onto something. Faith can occur only by means of the message concerning the Savior. If we want to say it in a catchy way, the Word is a given in the election for heaven!

Two passages in particular draw attention to God using his tools, or channels, of the means of grace to bring us to faith and make us his own. Notice how Paul speaks in each of these verses of the way in which the Holy Spirit caused us to believe in Christ so that we would be among the elect. The first is Ephesians 1:13: "You also were included in Christ when you heard the word of truth, the gospel of your salvation." The second is 1 Thessalonians 1:4,5: "We know, brothers loved by God, that he has chosen you, because our gospel came to you not simply with words, but also with power, with the Holy Spirit and with deep conviction."

The connections among our election, faith, and the means of grace are made especially clear in this latter verse. A more literal translation would be, "We know, brothers loved by God, of your election, because our gospel did not come about for you in speech only but also in connection with power and in connection with the Holy Spirit and with much absolute assurance." The Holy Spirit powerfully carries out our election as he uses the gospel to work faith. To paraphrase Paul, "Seeing that the gospel has worked faith in you, this is why we realize you are to be considered among the elect."

Doesn't Paul answer the question that may trouble all of us from time to time? We may wonder, "In this vast world filled with billions of people, how can I—a lowly sinner—be confident without a doubt that I stand among the elect? I look around and see that not all who hear about Christ are believers. Does this mean I could be deceiving myself when I count my soul among the elect?" To this Paul would reply, "You can know you are included with the chosen ones by faith in the gospel because the Spirit's power brings conviction to the heart through the gospel."

In response to a related question submitted by a reader of the *Lutheran Sentinel* column "Pastor, I Have a Question," this answer was given:

> As long as one hears the Gospel, which tells of the unconditional love of God toward all sinners in sending Christ to pay for all sins, there is always hope for heaven. There is no salvation, there is no election or predestination *apart from* hearing the Gospel as God presents it to hearts of sinners in Word and Sacrament. Faith in Christ, which is absolutely necessary for one to have eternal life, is always worked in an individual only through Baptism and the message of God's Word. This is how the forgiveness of sins won by Christ is brought to the unconverted soul, enabling the Holy Spirit to do

his work. . . . This is the only way that the Christian
takes comfort in this mysterious teaching.[8]

Writing to a Christian who was plagued by doubt and
uncertainty about his election and salvation, Martin
Luther gave this spiritual counsel:

> God has given us his Son, Jesus Christ, whom we should
> remember every day and to whom we should look as in a
> mirror. For outside of Christ there is only danger, death
> and devil, but in him everything is peace and joy. Whoso-
> ever is constantly tormented by the predestination wins
> nothing else than fear. Therefore avoid and flee these
> thoughts that look like Satan's temptation in paradise,
> and, instead of that, look at Christ.[9]

By his advice to look to Christ, Luther urged his troubled friend to do the same thing Paul urges: Find refuge
in the *gospel*. There alone the Holy Spirit busily creates
and strengthens the very faith by which God brings about
our election.

We cannot emphasize this truth enough. By nature our
sinful hearts do not want to rely only upon the Word for
having faith and the assurance of our election. Like the
Jews who demanded miraculous signs and the Greeks who
were looking for wisdom (1 Corinthians 1:22), our human
nature is inclined to probe other avenues for obtaining
assurance instead of God's avenue of simple faith in the
gospel promises. Could one of those alternate avenues be
our emotions? If we *feel* like good Christians, should this
make us more sure of our election? Our emotions, our per-
ceptions, and our suppositions can deceive us. In fact,
Luther went so far as to say, "Whatever is attributed to the
Spirit apart from such Word and sacrament is of the
devil."[10] Faith that rests solely on *God's Word* cannot

God has chosen me to be his own from eternity

His electing me is all by his mercy poured out in Christ's work of atonement

God's way of electing me is only through the use of his Word and sacraments

God's Holy Spirit brings my sinful heart to believe in Christ and preserves me in faith deceive, because God himself, who has given these words, cannot lie. He is the one who says, "Everyone who looks to the Son and believes in him shall have eternal life, and I will raise him up at the last day" (John 6:40).

Before we move on, let's briefly recap:

- If faith saves,

- if God himself works the faith that saves,

- if God's election is only through faith, and

- if faith comes about only through the Word,

then faith must only and always be God's own action in us.

God's work entirely

Imagine the following scenario: You receive a check in the mail for one million dollars. The explanation given is that this gift has been intended for you even before the time you were born. Amazingly, nothing was demanded of you in order to have this gift. To receive its benefits you were to go to the bank and cash the check. No doubt you would have questions: Is it really genuine and legitimate? Is it a mistake—a gift meant for someone else? Is it backed by the necessary funds and authority? But you go to the bank and cash it. You find out it is indeed a genuine gift, and the money is placed into your account!

Would it be proper for you to think later, "I received the money because I did not treat the check as junk mail but willingly went to the bank and cashed it"? The check was a gift from start to finish. You received the benefit of the gift through making the trip to the bank. Nothing on your part caused the generous benefactor to make the gift. You just cashed in on it!

We might speak of faith in Christ as the way to cash in on the inheritance check of our eternal election. Oh, someone might say: "Well, *we* are the ones who believe, aren't we? If the person in the illustration had to go to the bank and cash the check in order for the gift to be effective, can't we say the same about faith in Christ?"

The difference is this: God himself is the one who drives us to the bank! God himself is the one who has us cash in on his gift! God's plan of salvation for individual people is from start to finish all his work. Whether we speak of his electing us, his bringing us to faith by the means of grace, our continuing in the faith until death, or our departing from this world to heaven, we believers know each phase along the way is due completely to the efforts of our divine benefactor. The apostle Paul told the Philippian Christians they were to be confident of this: "He who began a good work in you will carry it on to completion until the day of Christ Jesus" (1:6).

Some insist that God expects cooperation by sinners in their salvation. For example, they often misunderstand two important verses: Revelation 3:20, "Here I am! I stand at the door and knock. If anyone hears my voice and opens the door, I will come in and eat with him, and he with me," and Philippians 2:12, "Continue to work out your salvation with fear and trembling."

Philippians 2:12 is not speaking of conversion. It refers to the Christian's life of sanctification and addresses how one makes use of the Word and sacraments in daily life. This is no light matter for, after conversion, Christians easily lose sight of spiritual matters. Even though orthodox Lutheran theologians have always upheld cooperation by the believer in sanctification, they have consistently condemned any such cooperation in conversion. The very next verse of Philippians shows where the credit belongs even in the Christian's life of sanctification: "It is God who works in you to will and to act according to his good purpose" (verse 13).

In response to Revelation 3:20, we treat this passage the same way we look at all Scripture verses that tell us to believe. We call these "gospel invitations" or "gospel commands." In other words, the very thing God asks us to do (namely, open the door, believe, and so on), he himself supplies us with the ability to do. When we say, "I believe in Christ," we are acknowledging that God the Holy Spirit has led us to take hold of the Savior for our forgiveness and eternal life. We read in 2 Corinthians 4:6, "God . . . made his light shine in our hearts."

The fact that our election is God's work entirely is expressed in our Lutheran Confessions:

> He saves us "according to the purpose" of his will through sheer mercy in Christ without our merit and good works, as it is written, "He destined us in love to be his sons through Jesus Christ, according to the purpose of his will, and to the praise of his glorious grace which he freely bestowed upon us in the Beloved" (Ephesians 1:5,6). It is therefore false and wrong when men teach that the cause of our election is not only the mercy of God and the most holy merit of Christ, but that there is also within us a cause of God's election on account of which God has elected us unto eternal life.[11]

Our election is realized through faith in Christ, worked through the means of grace. God the Holy Spirit is the active agent in resurrecting our naturally dead souls to seize new life in Christ. The Spirit's tools for this tremendous work of spiritual resurrection are Holy Baptism and the gospel.

Numerous errors related to election would never have arisen if the biblical teaching of the means of grace would have been permitted to stand pure and untouched. Election to eternal life includes faith in Christ. Faith in Christ includes the means of grace. And using the means of grace includes the work of God the Holy Spirit, without whom we could never speak of our inclusion among the elect.

Since God carries out our election to eternal life only by means of his Word and sacraments, we can now proceed to discuss even further our election security.

5

Our Election Assurance

As with any teaching of Scripture, we need to ask ourselves, "Why do I want to learn what the Bible teaches about election?" Just as we should not look into the mystery of our Lord's virgin birth nor peer into the doctrine of the Holy Trinity apart from wanting to be strengthened in our faith, so also our purpose for studying election is to be strengthened in our faith. Although some may think of election as little more than a topic for debates by philosophers and skeptics, this doctrine brings comfort to Christians, who know they have been purchased by the blood of Christ and that God truly wants them to be his children now and forever.

We have already mentioned that the teaching of election in Romans follows right after Paul's thorough exposition of how a sinner is justified before God. In a heart-warming way, Paul offers election for the believer's confidence: "Who will bring any charge against those whom God has chosen? It is God who justifies. Who is he that condemns? Christ Jesus, who died—more than that, who was raised to life—is at the right hand of God and is also interceding for us. Who shall separate us from the love of Christ?" (8:33-35). It is evident from Paul's presentation that the purpose of election is to give believers in Christ *assurance for time and eternity.* We touched on this point earlier, but two reasons compel us to pursue this in a separate chapter: (1) Our *need* for being assured that we are of the elect is a constant one. (2) Since election is often misunderstood, such a misunderstanding can easily lead to spiritual confusion and doubt.

I must confess that as a young boy in confirmation class, I had a difficult time seeing how this teaching could be assuring. My pastor reminded me that when we think about election, we need to focus on faith in Christ. So if God says only believers in Christ make up the elect, then the personal question must be, "Do I right now, by God's grace, believe in Jesus as my Savior?"

True, a person may fall from faith and therefore not be one of the elect. Should this make me worry? More to the point, *does* this make me worry? Satan, who is so clever that he even masquerades as an angel of light (2 Corinthians 11:14), tries hard to shake me from my faith. But when the temptation to doubt creeps into my mind, I need to remind myself that election is always *in Christ.* I need to zero in on Christ, not myself. I need to hear how election reminds me: Through faith, you are in Christ, so you are to know you are among the elect. Remain in Jesus' saving grace for the duration of your life, giving careful attention to the means of grace, and you will one day be with all of the elect gathered by the angels into the heavenly kingdom of God! (Mark 13:27).

What if personal questions arise?

Satan is an accuser. That's what his name means. He loves to bring charges against the children of God. He is delighted when he can plant worry, doubt, and despair in the minds of Christians. Our old sinful flesh helps him. It too raises disturbing questions. "If you call yourself one of the elect children of God," it argues, "why do you keep sinning? How can you be so sure—as you say you are— that you are among God's chosen ones? Wouldn't his chosen ones be more faithful to God in their daily living?"

In this connection, George Stoeckhardt, a 19th-century Lutheran seminary professor, offered some sound advice in his commentary on Romans 8:

> Christians do have enemies who accuse them. They are all hostile powers, as Satan, the world and the flesh. . . . Christians are not yet without guilt. We daily sin much against the law of God. These sins and transgressions Satan, the real accuser, brings before God's tribunal. Our fellowmen complain that we have often and grievously offended them. Our own conscience condemns us as guilty. However, these accusations are weak.[12]

How can Stoeckhardt say these accusations are weak? He goes on to explain:

> For the apostle calls the accused "the elect from God." God has chosen them from the world, from the lost masses. . . . God, who is the judge in this matter, gives no ear to the accusation against His elect but *pronounces upon them an absolving judgment.* He absolves them from their transgressions and forgives them all their sins daily and

richly for His Son's sake, whom He gave into death for
them as a propitiation [atoning sacrifice] for their guilt.[13]

Satan also assails us from other angles. He may tempt
us to travel the route of spiritual arrogance. Playing on
our sinful minds, he can raise questions like these: "The
elect will be brought into eternal life. Now if I am one
of the elect, why do I need to be so careful every step
along the way? After all, God is going to save me. So
won't he do everything necessary before my time expires
to turn me around? Won't he keep me from rolling head-
long down the wrong path, even if I veer sideways once
in a while?"

We must address the apparent conflict between the following teachings of Scripture:

- A person can fall away from faith.

- A person can be sure of his or her election.

When the Bible mentions the risk of losing our faith,
this doesn't destroy the assurance election gives to us.
Caution against falling from faith is directed at our old
sinful nature, not against our new nature in Christ. Such
caution is a severe preaching of the law. But the assurance
for a Christian that he or she is one of the elect is never
based on the law, but only the gospel. Certainty of salvation for the Christian always is related to the promise of
God's forgiveness in Christ. This is how the Holy Spirit
accomplishes his work. Christians can then know they
will receive everlasting life as long as they rely on the
gospel. In short, believers know they are not beyond the
temptation to fall, but they find security for their personal
election in God's truth, which never fails. Let's explore
this thought further.

Security in the Word

Scripture gives security, solid hope, to sinners in its message of salvation through faith in Jesus Christ. "For everything that was written in the past was written to teach us, so that through endurance and the encouragement of the Scriptures we might have hope" (Romans 15:4).

God's Word is not just a record of history. It holds the power of God himself. It brings people to faith and secures them in that faith until eternity. To direct doubting souls to any other source for strength is foolishness.

Preachers who tell their people, "If you want greater assurance of your salvation, then pay closer attention to how you conduct your lives as Christians" or "Your election is made more secure by the strength of your personal faith" are doing their people no favors. For in both cases, the basis for security is false.

Let's explain. Whenever I imagine that being sure of my salvation or election depends on something in me or something I do, I don't find the assurance I need. I am taking my eyes off of Christ and what he did for me, and instead, I'm looking at myself. Even the fact that I strive with God's help to follow his will and live a Christian life is not a sufficient basis for being absolutely sure of my salvation. I'm still a sinner, and sometimes my sinful nature gets the best of me. I think, say, and do things that God's holy law condemns. My Christian life is far from perfect and therefore not a sure basis for the hope I need to have for eternal life. But Christ's life for me is! The life he lived for me was perfect. His death for me paid for all my sins. His resurrection for me is an unassailable fact. What Christ did for me alone provides the assurance I need for my salvation. What Christ did for me is an objective truth that never changes. "Jesus Christ is the same yesterday and today and forever" (Hebrews 13:8). How can God ever deny a sinner strength and salvation when the sinner cries, "Just as I am, without one plea but that thy blood was shed for me" (CW 397:1)?

Yes, the blood of *God himself* shed at Calvary always gives security. There's nothing questionable about our forgiveness then, for we were redeemed "with the precious blood of Christ, a lamb without blemish or defect" (1 Peter 1:19). When your sins trouble you and get you to doubt that you are one of the elect, hold firmly to the gospel which proclaims that Christ has redeemed all people and whoever believes in him shall not perish but have everlasting life.

Dr. P. E. Kretzmann penned this advice years ago:

> If ever any doubt as to our salvation wants to rise in our hearts, then we should remember and cling to the knowledge that God from eternity has taken the matter of our salvation and all that pertains to it into His merciful and powerful hand. In the midst of all crosses and trials, when it would seem that God has abandoned us entirely, we should rest our faith upon His Word, which tells us that all the tribulations of this present time are but incidents along the way to heaven, and can in no way compare with the glory which shall be revealed in us on the day of our final redemption.[14]

Christians can and should be sure of their election. "Faith is being sure of what we hope for and certain of what we do not see" (Hebrews 11:1). Anyone who contends that Christians cannot be certain of their election is promoting error. Believers will have doubts, for they remain both saints and sinners until they depart from this world. But to suggest that a level of uncertainty about one's election possibly is virtuous and a sign of God-pleasing humility is at the height of deception! God wants us to take him at his word. His Son is "the atoning sacrifice for our sins, and not only for ours but also for the sins of the whole world" (1 John 2:2). He tells all to believe this. And then he insists, "There is now no condemnation for those who are in Christ Jesus" (Romans 8:1). There's not a trace of doubt in the message of God's gospel to us! Dare we ever raise any questions about his promises? Through faith in Christ, Paul reminds all of us how unshakable our confidence can be: "I am convinced that neither death nor life, neither angels nor demons, neither the present nor the future, nor any powers, neither height nor depth, nor anything else in all creation, will be able to separate us from the love of God that is in Christ Jesus our Lord" (Romans 8:38,39).

Other foundations are shaky and will give way. When our consciences continually remind us of our sins and failures, we need to grasp the impregnable rock that will endure when all else fails. God is our immovable Gibraltar. His message of redemption through the blood of his Son is a mountain of solid granite, majestically rising above all the clouds of life and defying all the ravages of time. No, it's more than a mountain! God had Isaiah state it this way: "'Though the mountains be shaken and the hills be removed, yet my unfailing love for you will not be shaken nor my covenant of peace be removed,' says the LORD, who has compassion on you" (Isaiah 54:10).

Loving warnings need to be sounded

After stressing the assurance and comfort of one's election given through the nonretractable promises of God, we must also—for the good of our faith—observe some warnings. The warnings are necessary because we remain both saints and sinners until we die. God gives these warnings in sincere love for our souls.

The often-used admonition "Pride goes before the fall" applies to those who would think that because they believe in Christ today and are certain of their election, their guard against sin and unbelief can come down. Election assurance does not mean we can adopt an attitude of indifference toward the gospel. "Cheap grace" thinking (the feeling that pious living is not important because grace alone saves) has no place in the life of a believer. Peter warned his hearers of this when he wrote, "Therefore, my brothers, be all the more eager to make your calling and election sure" (2 Peter 1:10). Conscientious use of God's Word for our faith and lives is a must. In the same chapter, Peter notes, "We have the word of the prophets made more certain, and you will do well [the Greek actually says "you *are* doing well"] to pay attention to it" (verse 19).

If anyone gets away from the Word or becomes careless in leading a life based on the Word, of what benefit is election security? In his book on Christian doctrine, Edward Koehler says: "We find comfort in our election only while we are in the faith. Hence, to make our election sure to ourselves, we must give diligence that we remain steadfast in the faith. To this end we must make use of those means by which God assures us of His grace and thereby of our election."[15]

Another matter to consider is this: Human reason insists that election inevitably leads a person to fatalism. It argues: "If a person isn't elected, there's no chance; so why care how you live? You will be damned if you do and damned if you don't!" But human reason fails to see the power of God's grace in election. That power bringing his love to our souls transcends all reason! When we learn about election in Scripture, God's powerful love is at work. By telling us we have been picked for heaven by his grace—even from eternity—he is using his power to bring confidence to our hearts.

Yes, God has chosen us to be his very own from eternity! Is there any greater news for you and me to hear? He didn't only pay the penalty for our sins with the substitutionary sacrifice of his Son. He didn't only call us to be his own. He didn't only bring us to faith by the power of his Spirit. Before time began, he chose us to inherit everlasting life by making us his dear heirs!

We believers long to serve our Lord in thankfulness and join Peter in exulting:

> Praise be to the God and Father of our Lord Jesus Christ! In his great mercy he has given us new birth into a living hope through the resurrection of Jesus Christ from the dead, and into an inheritance that can never perish, spoil or fade—kept in heaven for you, who through faith are shielded by God's power until the coming of the salvation that is ready to be revealed in the last time. (1 Peter 1:3-5)

Our election gives us assurance because it drives us to the Word, where we are told that, through Christ's saving work, places in heaven have been reserved for us believers. To use an illustration, imagine that you have reserved seats to a sporting event or theatrical production. While a crowd gathers in the ticket line, you know you will be admitted because you have your ticket in hand. You *will* be admitted. The analogy clearly limps, but picture the sense of security we have in knowing that Christ has won reserved places for us in heaven. He has chosen us prior to any setting of the stage. And he has given us the document of this guaranteed reservation in the form of the Holy Bible. In the

Bible Jesus declares: "In my Father's house are many rooms; if it were not so, I would have told you. I am going there to prepare a place for you. And if I go and prepare a place for you, I will come back and take you to be with me that you also may be where I am" (John 14:2,3).

6

Our Election Is Entirely by Grace

Grace is the attitude behind the gift placed into the hand of a beggar. No beggar earns the gift by what he or she does. The gift comes from the heart of a generous benefactor. God is our benefactor. We sinners are beggars who have nothing to offer or use as a bargaining chip with God. Rather, we are saved entirely by God's grace, his undeserved love freely given. The passage "He saved us, not because of righteous things we had done, but because of his mercy" (Titus 3:5) applies to every detail of our salvation, including especially how God elected us from eternity. Our Lord Jesus told his followers, "You did not choose me, but I chose you" (John 15:16).

To illustrate this concept, we might use the example of citizenship in the United States. We who were born in the

USA consider ourselves fortunate. What did we have to do with this? What did we do to obtain this privilege? Was there some sort of "quality" difference in our human make-up that influenced God to put us in this bountiful land rather than in some famine-ravaged country of the Third World? The thought is absurd! Neither did our American citizenship depend on the good qualities of our ancestors. The only reason we were born as American citizens is God's grace!

Carry the thought a step farther. We poor sinners were brought to faith in Christ by God's eternal plan in order that we might be citizens in his everlasting kingdom. "Our citizenship is in heaven. And we eagerly await a Savior from there, the Lord Jesus Christ" (Philippians 3:20). But this citizenship, bestowed upon us by the new birth of Baptism and the Word, does not depend on any quality of goodness within ourselves. It comes only as a gift from our merciful Creator. So we say emphatically, *Our election is entirely by grace!*

The causes of election

Some speak of *two* causes of our election: God's grace and the merits of Christ. We can speak this way because Scripture does. In reality these two are basically *one*: God's grace in Christ.

The following Scripture verses speak of God's grace as the cause of our election: "[God] has saved us and called us to a holy life—not because of anything we have done but because of his own purpose and grace" (2 Timothy 1:9). (The Greek word for "grace" carries the thought of free giving. Grace is always a gift to which a person has no claim on the basis of merit.) We read in Romans 9:11,12 that "God's purpose in election might stand: not by works but by him who calls." And two chapters later, Paul speaks of "a remnant chosen by grace" (11:5).

Scripture also speaks of Christ's merits as the cause for our election. We covered this important point earlier. Yet mindful of the fact that some still maintain that a good quality in humans influences God's election decision, we need to emphasize once more how the Bible distinctly links our election always to Christ. When the following passages say we are chosen *in Christ*, this is another way of saying: "Dear believer, never be confused as to *why* you are among the chosen: You have been chosen only because of Christ's merits. No goodness within yourself ever formed the basis for God's election. When God says 'in Christ,' this is another way of stressing his grace—grace displayed in Christ's cross."

> This grace was given us in Christ Jesus before the beginning of time. (2 Timothy 1:9)
>
> For he chose us in him before the creation of the world . . . according to his eternal purpose which he accomplished in Christ Jesus our Lord. (Ephesians 1:4; 3:11)

Since Christ lived a holy life in the place of every sinner and also died as the substitutionary sacrifice for the penalty of all sins, his grace covers all people. "God was reconciling the world to himself in Christ" (2 Corinthians 5:19). We also know God wants every single person to be saved. Peter writes, "The Lord . . . is patient with you, not wanting anyone to perish, but everyone to come to repentance" (2 Peter 3:9).

To our human reason there certainly seems to be a contradiction between universal grace (God wants all people to be saved and Christ died to redeem all people) and particular election (God has elected only particular individuals to eternal salvation). We do not try to solve the apparent contradiction; rather, we let stand the clear truths of Scripture without trying to reconcile them to human reason. God sincerely wants all people to be saved. God gets all the credit for those who are saved. Our Lutheran Confessions state:

> The reason why "many are called and few are chosen" is not that in his call, which takes place through the Word, God intended to say: "Externally I do indeed through the Word call all of you, to whom I give my Word, into my kingdom, but down in my heart I am not thinking of all, but only of a certain few."[16]

When a person is lost, this is not God's fault. He sincerely wants all to be saved. When a person is lost, the Bible places the blame squarely on sinful, human resistance of the Spirit's work. "You stiff-necked people . . . you always resist the Holy Spirit" (Acts 7:51).

But someone may say: "Doesn't God know all things? Doesn't he know who will ultimately be saved and who will be lost?" Yes, God surely knows all things, even those who will be lost (1 John 3:20). A vital distinction needs to be made, however, between God's foreknowledge—his omniscience, which covers all things—and his predestination of souls. His foreknowledge covers all people. But predestination applies only to believers, according to the Bible's own restrictions. In other words, although God certainly knows who will be saved and who will not, this does not take away from his universal grace, nor does it mean he predestines any to damnation.

All this leads each of us to ask a very important personal question: "Why am I a believer?" You and I can only answer, "God has chosen me by grace through the merits of Christ." To say anything else—for example, to speak about our personal faith as the cause—destroys election and salvation only by God's grace. We who believe in Christ should exclaim, "By the grace of God I am what I am" (1 Corinthians 15:10). There is no other cause involved in our election. When anyone suggests that in eternity God foresaw who would believe or who would have a nobler character or less resistance and elected those individuals on that basis, this maligns God's grace and Christ's work. If we attribute our election—even by a tiny percent—to a cause other than what is listed in Scripture, we join the ranks of those who teach salvation by works, not grace.

Original sin's impact

Whenever anyone speaks of a cause for election besides God's grace and Christ's merit—in other words, some third cause in humans—you can be sure the effects of original sin are being downplayed. The Bible, by contrast, makes terribly crushing statements about the natural spiritual condition of every human being:

> The sinful mind is hostile to God. It does not submit to God's law, nor can it do so. (Romans 8:7)

> Like the rest, we were by nature objects of wrath. (Ephesians 2:3)

> "Every inclination of his heart is evil from childhood." (Genesis 8:21)

> I know that nothing good lives in me, that is, in my sinful nature. (Romans 7:18)

> Surely I was sinful at birth, sinful from the time my mother conceived me. (Psalm 51:5)

From conception and birth, all people would experience eternal condemnation in hell if God had not dealt with the conditions prevailing since the fall of Adam and Eve. The apostle Paul speaks to this very point. He casts the entire world under the pall of God's wrath because of Adam's sin and says, "The result of one trespass was condemnation for all men" (Romans 5:18).

Many rebel against the doctrine of original sin because they do not like the necessary conclusions it draws for their personal lives. But who does? When Scripture places humanity under such severe censure, an alarm bell sounds for *all*. The Lutheran Confessions state that God's purpose in doing so is "to make original sin manifest and show man to what utter depths his nature has fallen and how corrupt it has become."[17] God's purpose is to drive from our hearts all false hopes and useless illusions in order to direct us to the true and lasting hope—a hope we find only in the gospel, which tells of Christ's saving grace.

Rebuking the Pharisees who criticized him for eating with "tax collectors and sinners," Jesus said, "It is not the healthy who need a doctor, but the sick" (Matthew 9:12). Think of a patient who tells her physician, "I'm not really sick," even though she's lying at death's door and the doctor could prescribe a medicine to cure her. Such a person needs to be convinced of the seriousness of her illness and has to see it as real before she feels the need to grab the medicine bottle. In a similar way, only when people realize the eternally terminal effects of original sin upon their lives will the medicine of Christ's gospel be appreciated.

What does this have to do with looking upon our election in the light of God's mercy? Plenty. Only when original sin is misunderstood or denied could someone propose the idea that some good quality in humans influences God's decision to choose them. If that is the case, if something good within people influences God, then God's grace stops being grace. Confusion on this isn't merely of little consequence. Eternal consequences are at stake! God's grace is at the heart and center of election's assurance and comfort. If we were to teach that God elects people because of something good he foresaw in them, we would fall into the same error as the Roman Catholic Church, mixing good works into the way of salvation. But Scripture answers emphatically, "It is by grace you have been saved, through faith—and this not from yourselves, it is the gift of God—not by works, so that no one can boast" (Ephesians 2:8,9).

The Lutheran reformers held that the spiritual corruption of original sin is so penetrating that "it is something that has to be learned and believed from the revelation of Scriptures."[18] In fact, the reformers condemned in the strongest terms the false teachings that "original sin is only an external impediment to man's good spiritual powers and not the complete deprivation or loss of the same" and that "this blemish may be removed as readily as a spot can be washed from the face or color from the wall."[19]

Only God's grace keeps us certain

God's election is intended for our comfort and assurance. But God's election keeps us sure of our salvation only when we hold fast to the scriptural truth that his mercy—and nothing else—has influenced his choosing of our souls to have eternal life.

In Romans 9 Paul used the story of Jacob and Esau to illustrate the fact that everything depends on the merciful choice of God and not on anything else, such as one's physical descent from Abraham. Paul wrote: "Rebekah's children had one and the same father, our father Isaac. Yet, before the twins were born or had done anything good or bad—in order that God's purpose in election might stand: not by works but by him who calls—she was told, 'The older will serve the younger'" (verses 10-12).

Recall the account in Genesis. Rebekah was pregnant with twins. Feeling the movement of the babies in her womb, she asked the Lord what it meant. He answered her: "Two nations are in your womb, and two peoples from within you will be separated; one people will be stronger than the other, and the older will serve the younger" (Genesis 25:23). God had chosen Jacob's descendants to be his special people, the heirs of the messianic promises, even though Esau was the older of the twins.

The point Paul makes in connection with election is this: From eternity God in his mercy had planned to make Jacob's descendants (the Israelites) his own special people so that from that nation all nations of the world would be blessed. By electing Jacob, God designated him to be the heir of the messianic promise. This was, as Paul says, "not by works but by him who calls" (Romans 9:12). In other words, God had not chosen Jacob for this privilege because he foresaw Jacob would be much better than Esau; God chose Jacob simply by mercy. (After all, Jacob also showed a dark side in his acts of deception.) The apostle draws the comparison to the entire matter of election and salvation and then draws this conclusion: "It does not, therefore, depend on man's desire or effort, but on God's mercy" (Romans 9:16).

How tragic it would be if we were ever led to believe that our election was not entirely by God's grace! Anything we then would try to hang our hopes on would give way. There is no other place for sinners to have assurance than Jesus' blood and righteousness, the full grace of God!

Just as God elected Jacob to have the birthright blessing purely by his grace prior to Jacob's birth, so God elected us to have eternal life entirely by his grace before we were born into this world. His grace brought us to faith in Christ through Baptism. Since our election is based completely on his grace and not on the slightest bit of merit on our part, we can say: "My election is sure! I am saved! Nothing can keep me from having heaven, for Christ's grace and merits alone count! And when I cling to that, who can bring any charge against me?"

7

Our Election:
Errors before and after the Reformation

We obtain God's absolute truth for our lives only through what he has revealed to us in the pages of Holy Scripture. "All Scripture is God-breathed and is useful for teaching, rebuking, correcting and training in righteousness" (2 Timothy 3:16). This is true for all doctrines of the Christian faith, including election. In fact, if any part of the doctrine of election were to rest on human opinion and not entirely on the Word of God, the foundation for our hope surely would crumble. But Christ's church on earth does not wish to build on any other foundation than that of "the apostles and prophets"—the inspired and inerrant words God gave the holy writers—"with Christ Jesus himself as the chief cornerstone" (Ephesians 2:20).

Human reason loves trying to supply answers to questions and scenarios left unanswered in Scripture. For example, the Bible does not provide a logically consistent answer to the question "Why are some saved and not others?" Human reason sees this as a challenge to furnish its answers. Religious leaders who have tried to answer this puzzling question have led their hearers down the spiritually treacherous paths of synergism, false security, and despair. Synergism falsely teaches that salvation comes through a certain amount of cooperation by the human will along with God's free grace. False security happens when sinners seeks their confidence for salvation in something other than the gospel promises in Scripture. Despair is the hopeless abandonment that comes when a sinner loses sight of Christ's cross as the way to heaven.

God's truth versus human opinion
Ever since Adam and Eve fell into sin in the Garden of Eden, sinners have attempted to lean on their own understanding rather than rely solely on God's revealed truth. Eve was intrigued by the devil's challenging question, "Did God really say . . ." (Genesis 3:1). She seemed fascinated by Satan's implication that she knew better than God concerning the forbidden fruit.

Scripture is filled with people who have raised the question "Did God really say?" Although Noah was a "preacher of righteousness" (2 Peter 2:5) who warned the people of his day about the coming flood, they did not listen. They insisted they knew better. What could Noah's God tell them that they could not gather by using their own senses and reason? What was the result for those scoffers? Jesus says: "In the days before the flood, people were eating and drinking, marrying and giving in marriage, up to the day Noah entered the ark; and they knew nothing about what would happen until the flood came and took them all away" (Matthew 24:38,39).

Consider the days of Jeremiah. The people of Judah heard the prophet predict exactly what the Lord had revealed to him: Judah's inhabitants would be taken into captivity by the Babylonians. Yet they refused to believe God's message. They would not accept such doom, for it did not seem *reasonable*. But 70 years of captivity did indeed come, just as Jeremiah had spoken.

How did Zechariah react when the angel Gabriel announced that he and his wife, Elizabeth, would have a son? Reason told him: "There must be some mistake. My wife and I are too old to have children!" But nine months later—as you well know—God gave them a son, John the Baptist, who would "go on before the Lord to prepare the way for him" (Luke 1:76). Zechariah learned how reason cannot be trusted when it conflicts with the powerful Word from God.

Fallen humanity in its warped thinking has made a god out of reason at the expense of God's Word. Our Lord has told us that as a sign of the end times, "many will turn away from the faith" (Matthew 24:10). Many will reject the Word in favor of human opinions. The apostle Paul warned Timothy: "The time will come when men will not put up with sound doctrine. Instead, to suit their own desires, they will gather around them a great number of teachers to say what their itching ears want to hear" (2 Timothy 4:3).

This very thing has happened in connection with election. Some in the history of Christianity have turned their itching ears to listen to what appeals to human reason and have, either wittingly or unwittingly, abandoned the sound words of Scripture.

Dr. Luther and the early Lutheran reformers did not try to answer those questions where God had not revealed the answer. The Lutheran confessors held:

> Because God has reserved this mystery [here, the question "Who is going to heaven and who is going to hell?"] to his wisdom and not revealed anything concerning it in the Word, still less has commanded us to explore it through our speculations but has earnestly warned against it (Romans 11:33), therefore we are not, on the basis of our speculations, to make our own deductions, draw conclusions, or brood over it, but cling solely to his revealed Word, to which he directs us.[20]

Why Are Some Saved and Not Others?		
	Why are some saved?	*Why are others lost?*
Augustine Calvin	God's will	God's will
Semi-Pelagians Synergists	human will	human will
Luther Scripture	God's will	human will

Election in pre-Reformation days

In the fifth century A.D. election became the subject of much controversy. A monk named Pelagius denied original sin, taught salvation by good works, and insisted human beings have a free will in spiritual matters. In effect, he was saying people are capable of saving themselves. His views were adopted by some in the Roman church. Ultimately this led to the Pelagian Controversy. The debate centered on Pelagius' premise that Adam's sin affected only himself and did not carry over to the rest of the human race.

Augustine (A.D. 354–430), the bishop of Hippo, in North Africa, led a charge against Pelagius and had his teachings condemned. Augustine's efforts squelched Pelagianism until the time Pelagius died.

A new form of Pelagius' errors developed, however, known as semi-Pelagianism. (The Roman Catholic Church today contains elements reflecting the influence of this heresy.) Augustine also battled with the semi-Pelagians, who taught that human free will is only partially impaired by the fall into sin but still has enough strength to start pleasing God. Yet, they said, this will is not strong enough to go all the way to perfection. A person still needs God's grace to help along to salvation. God's grace helps a person's will. Semi-Pelagians also taught that the reason some are saved and others are not is found in an inner condition and manner of spiritual reception by each person: Some make the right use of their free will, while others do not.

In the theological debates that followed, a touch of irony developed. Augustine, who had refuted semi-Pelagianism as antiscriptural, himself fell into error's tangled web. To that inscrutable question "Why are some saved and not others?" Augustine proposed that God does not treat all alike with his grace. He taught that some people are saved because God predestined them to eternal life and others are lost because God predestined them to eternal death.

Years went by. Not only did the error of semi-Pelagianism persist, so did Augustine's error of double predestination. Both doctrines festered until the time of the Reformation.

Calvinism

At the same time Luther's reforms were taking place in Germany, Huldreich Zwingli (the founder of the Swiss Reformed church) was conducting an anti-Roman Catholic movement in Zurich. The man who succeeded Zwingli as the eminent thinker of the Swiss Reformed church was John Calvin (1509–1564) of Geneva. Calvin went on to become the most influential figure of the Reformed wing of the Protestant movement in Europe. Calvin supported the Augustinian view on predestination. He reasoned that if only some are elected to eternal life, it follows naturally that those who are rejected are lost because God himself did not desire to save them.

Since Calvin taught double predestination, an election *both* to heaven *and* hell, he also denied universal grace. Luther, his contemporary, simply upheld what the Bible says: Christ's death at the cross was "the atoning sacrifice for . . . the sins of the whole world" (1 John 2:2). But Calvin limited the effects of the atonement. He said God does not truly love all people, Christ's death paid the price only for the sins of believers, and the Holy Spirit is not interested in bringing all people to faith.

As a handy guide for understanding Calvinism, we find the acronym TULIP helpful. The following identifies the Reformed church as pioneered by John Calvin:

T *otal depravity*—Calvin taught that man is sinful from conception and birth and thus is lost by nature. (On this point, Lutherans also agree. *Arminian* Reformed groups, however, deny the full implications of original sin.

This Arminian idea has a strong influence among many Reformed churches today, including many Baptists.)

*U*nconditional election—Calvin taught double predestination: election both to heaven and hell. (Lutherans follow Scripture alone in saying God only has chosen some for eternal life through the means of grace.[21] Many Reformed, however, no longer follow Calvin's view on this.)

*L*imited atonement—Calvin taught that God never intended Christ's passion to save the whole world, but only those who believe. (Lutherans follow Scripture: John 1:29; 1 John 2:2; 2 Corinthians 5:15; and 2 Peter 2:1.)

*I*rresistible grace—Calvin taught that when the gospel invitation is extended to those who are not elected, God really doesn't desire that they repent and believe. God's grace is not really present for them. He also taught that when the gospel is extended to the elect, God compels them to come to faith through an irresistible "inner call." Therefore it can be said that God's grace is irresistible. (Lutherans confess that the grace of God truly desires the salvation of all when he calls people through the means of grace. This call can be and is rejected by those who do not believe.)

*P*erseverance of the saints—Calvin taught that the elect, once having received the Spirit, cannot again lose him entirely nor fall completely outside God's grace and ultimately be lost. (Lutherans follow God's Word, however, which teaches that believers may fall from faith and perish: Psalm 51:11; Hebrews 6:4-6; 10:26-29; Ezekiel 18:24; Luke 8:13,14; and 1 Timothy 1:19. Also, Romans 11:22-24 shows how faith is necessary until death in order to have elect status.)

A division developed among the early Calvinists. Some said that from eternity God *decreed* certain people to suffer

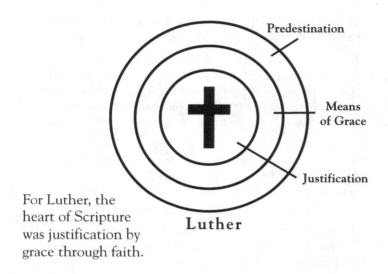

Predestination

Means
of Grace

Justification

For Luther, the
heart of Scripture
was justification by
grace through faith.

Luther

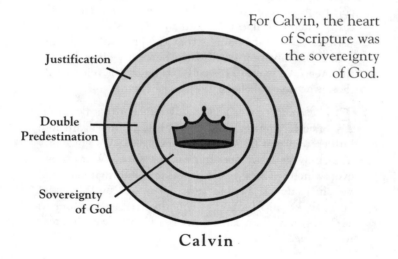

For Calvin, the heart
of Scripture was
the sovereignty
of God.

Justification

Double
Predestination

Sovereignty
of God

Calvin

The Approaches of Luther and Calvin to Theology

in hell. Another group had a similar belief, except for this slight difference: They said God simply *left* part of the human race under the curse of damnation, he merely passed by these people with his saving grace. In actuality both groups arrived at the same conclusion as Calvin: God, either more actively or passively, did not work as hard to rescue a large segment of people.

The Westminster Confession, the Presbyterian creed of 1647, espouses Calvin's theory of double predestination. The creed states, "By the decree of God, for the manifestation of his glory, some men and angels are predestinated unto everlasting life, and others foreordained to everlasting death."[22] Again, we find this remark: "The rest of mankind God was pleased, according to the unsearchable counsel of his own will, whereby he extendeth or withholdeth mercy as he pleaseth for the glory of his sovereign power over his creatures, to pass by and to ordain them to dishonor and wrath for their sin, to the praise of his glorious justice."[23]

For Calvin, God's sovereignty was the heart of Scripture. Therefore, Calvin held that if God in his absolute sovereignty predestined some people to salvation, he must have predestined others to damnation in the same way. To Calvin's way of thinking, anything else would have been logically inconsistent with God's sovereignty. But as Luther was quick to see, Calvin's logic was that of fallen humanity set on destroying God's objective justification, his act of reconciling the world to himself. For Luther, God's work of salvation in Christ was the heart of Scripture.

Philip Melanchthon

Luther remained faithful to Scripture in his teaching of election. The same cannot be said of all the other early

Lutherans. One of the first to waver on election was Luther's coworker Philip Melanchthon.

For Melanchthon, it seemed more important to be logically consistent in one's theology than faithful to the clear words of the Bible. Like Calvin, Melanchthon tried to answer the question "Why are some saved and not others?" by being logically consistent. Unlike Calvin, Melanchthon did affirm from Scripture that God's grace is universal and that he truly wants all people to be saved. But Melanchthon held to the idea of human free will in spiritual matters. He reasoned that if it is a person's own fault for rejecting Christ and being eternally lost, then (logically) those who are saved should receive at least some credit for their salvation. With free will, Melanchthon taught, some people choose to come to faith and be saved while others choose not to.

In connection with election, Melanchthon suggested that God in eternity foresaw something favorable in the hearts of some people (for example, God saw that certain hearts would be less resistant). Melanchthon felt constrained to answer the question "Why are some saved and not others?"—a question left unanswered by Scripture and also by Luther. In his famous book on Christian doctrine, Melanchthon wrote, "Since the promise is universal and since in God there are not conflicting wills, it is necessary that there is some cause within us for the difference as to why Saul is rejected and David received, that is, there must be a different action on the part of two men."[24]

You can imagine what an impact a man of Melanchthon's stature had on the Lutheran pastors in Germany. Because of his reputation as Luther's coworker, Melanchthon's views provided fuel for those who wanted to teach election in a "non-Lutheran" way. Those who fol-

lowed Melanchthon were known as Philippists and syner-
gists. (The word *synergist* defines anyone who believes sinners cooperate in some way in their conversion.)

Both Calvin's and Melanchthon's false teachings on
conversion and election were clearly rejected in the Formula of Concord, the last of the Lutheran Confessions,
contained in the *Book of Concord* of 1580.

Lutheran dogmaticians

Unfortunately, Lutheran troubles with election did not
come to an end with the clear, scriptural confession in the
Formula of Concord. A generation later, some Lutheran
dogmaticians (theological professors who taught classes on
Christian doctrine) started speaking of election in a way
that allowed error to creep in again. They spoke of God
electing people to salvation *in view of faith* (the Latin
expression was *intuitu fidei*). Among the influential
Lutheran dogmaticians who used this ambiguous phrase
was John Gerhard.

Gerhard's name in this connection may come as a sur-
prise. He has been called the 17th-century arch-theologian
of Lutheranism and was ardently opposed to all forms of
Calvinism. But in describing election, he unfortunately
used the "in view of faith" expression. Since this expression was being used in more than one way, a misunderstanding resulted. Some held that God elected people to
eternal life *in view of* (in the sense of *because of*) *faith* in
Christ, which God foresaw they would have. Others, like
Gerhard, talked about God's election of people *in view
of faith*, meaning simply that the elect are saved only by
being brought to faith in Christ during their lifetimes.
Calvinism had so stressed the sovereignty of God in election that faith in Christ looked rather superfluous.

Gerhard wished to connect election with faith. By using the "in view of faith" expression, however, he muddied the waters for a controversy yet to come.

Some Lutheran pastors adopted Gerhard's expression to imply they had the answer to the unanswerable "Why are some saved and not others?" How could they cave in on a point like this and weaken the meaning of God's grace? As you would expect, they still appealed to Scripture for their defense.

Where did these erring Lutheran leaders seek their scriptural support? They went to Romans 8. But look what happened when logic was placed above the bare Word. When they read verse 29, "For those God foreknew he also predestined," they interpreted the verse to say, "For those whose constant faith he foresaw he also predestined."[25] Even the renowned 17th-century theologian David Hollaz followed this approach. He remarked, "Predestination is the eternal decree of God to bestow eternal salvation upon all of whom God foresaw that they would finally believe in Christ."[26] In spite of how proper such a sentence may sound at first, it leaves room for a reason inside sinners as to why God chose them. This is a subtle departure from grace alone.

How should the phrase "For those God foreknew he also predestined" (Romans 8:29) be understood? Professor J. P. Meyer explained:

> Paul is not speaking about an experiment which God made in His omniscience before the creation of the world, and on the outcome of which He based His decision. . . . It is true, the syllable "fore" in "foreknow" dates God's knowledge back to eternity. But what does it mean when the Scriptures say that God "knows" some one? . . . Do not worry, he wants to say, in spite of your afflictions and weak-

nesses: did not God from eternity embrace you as His dear
children and clasp you to His bosom? Before you were born,
before you could do good or evil, before you could ever ask
Him any favor, He already claimed you as His own.[27]

As an example of the extent to which this "in view of
faith" expression was used, we observe that Danish theologian Erik Pontoppidan included it in his respectable cate-
chetical book *Sandhed til Gudfrygtighed* (*Truth Unto Godli-
ness*, 1737), which was widely used by Scandinavians to
instruct the youth in Luther's Small Catechism. An
answer to a question on election posed in his book reads,
"God has appointed all those to eternal life whom he from
eternity has seen would accept the grace proffered them,
believe in Jesus and persevere in this faith unto the end."[28]

The "in view of faith" expression found its way into the
1880s' election controversy among Lutherans in America.
Before proceeding to that controversy, we would do well
to ponder an important statement included in the Formula
of Concord. Its writers unequivocally *rejected* the following: "That it is not only the mercy of God and the most
holy merit of Christ, but that there is also within us a
cause of God's election, on account of which he has
elected us to eternal life."[29]

If only all Lutherans would have stuck with the position laid out in the Formula of Concord! If so, the next
controversy—almost exactly three hundred years after
the Formula's adoption—might never have occurred.

8

Our Election:
Errors in American Lutheranism

The election controversy in America had as much to do with the doctrine of conversion as with election. Crucial issues were at stake. What was the relationship of faith to election? Is the faith created in a sinner's heart by the Holy Spirit influenced by election, or does the person's faith have an influence on election? The scriptural answer is, "Faith flows from the election, and not election from faith."[30] Scripture speaks of our faith coming from God's election by grace. God doesn't elect in view of faith or because of faith. He elects *to* faith and *through* faith. In his Word he never speaks of our faith as a reason or cause of our election:

From the beginning God chose you to be saved through the sanctifying work of the Spirit and through belief in the truth. (2 Thessalonians 2:13)

All who were appointed for eternal life believed. (Acts 13:48)

C. F. W. Walther and F. A. Schmidt

For a brief history of this controversy among early Lutherans in America, we focus on the old Norwegian Synod. This synod, established in 1853 in southern Wisconsin, is the immediate forerunner of the current Evangelical Lutheran Synod (ELS), a church body in full doctrinal fellowship with the Wisconsin Evangelical Lutheran Synod (WELS). By 1872 the Norwegian Synod had formed a confessional alliance with the Missouri Synod, led by the prominent theologian Dr. C. F. W. Walther. The Wisconsin Synod and the Ohio Synod were also members of this alliance, called the Synodical Conference.

The newly formed Synodical Conference hoped to combine the theological training schools of the respective member synods. The seminary students would come under the direct supervision of the Synodical Conference. But the subsequent election controversy shattered all such hopes.

A professor from the Norwegian Synod, F. A. Schmidt, represented the Norwegian contingent at Concordia Seminary in St. Louis from 1872 to 1876. Schmidt had Missouri Synod roots and even had been confirmed by Walther. But after Walther gave an essay on election—an essay that properly stressed God's grace—Schmidt charged that Walther and the Missouri Synod were teaching Calvinistic errors on predestination and conversion. Schmidt maintained that a person is elected "in view of his or her faith" (*intuitu fidei*). Schmidt claimed Walther was disconnecting

God's election of sinners to salvation from faith in Christ needed for eternal life. Walther's omission of the "in view of faith" expression raised in Schmidt's eyes an old fear that faith was being discarded, leaving room open to teach an election of sinners without means.

Walther knew that men like Gerhard and Pontoppidan used the "in view of faith" expression. He acknowledged that they apparently didn't use the expression to imply human cooperation in salvation (synergism). But since others had used this phrase in that manner, Walther discouraged its use.

Schmidt's views fell mostly on deaf ears among pastors in the Missouri Synod and the Wisconsin Synod. He did find sympathy, however, among many in the Ohio Synod (which eventually left the Synodical Conference) and especially in his own Norwegian Synod. Schmidt's views caused so much division among the Norwegian Lutherans that congregations were split and relatives fought with relatives. Pastors were deposed in a number of congregations, and courts were flooded with lawsuits.

Schmidt's election error was, indeed, attractive to itching ears. He argued, "When only one of two ungodly men is converted, there must have been a difference in their resistance; for, if not, they would both have been converted."[31] Schmidt gained a following since his line of argument seemed logically convincing: If a person is converted, didn't this imply his or her will was less abrasive to God's call?

But no scriptural answer can be given as to why one is saved while another is condemned. Schmidt attempted to explain what the Bible does not explain. One church historian summed up the controversy with these two sentences: "The Synod's pastors put faith *after* election, bestowed upon the individual as a result of his election. Prof. Schmidt put faith *before* election, making it the *cause* of the individual's election."[32]

Walther used this illustration to emphasize the role faith plays:

> Faith is merely a passive instrument, like a hand into which some one places a dollar. The person receives the dollar provided he does not withdraw his hand; beyond that he does not have to do anything. The donor is doing the essential part by putting the gift into the hand, not the other party, by holding out the hand. Let a beggar approach a miser and see what his holding out of the hand to him will help him; the miser may set his dogs upon him if he annoys him too much.[33]

Walther's illustration coincides with the 14th thesis listed in his famous book *The Proper Distinction Between Law and Gospel*: "The Word of God is not rightly divided when faith is required *as a condition* of justification and salvation, as if a person were righteous in the sight of God and saved, not only by faith, but also *on account of his faith*, for the sake of his faith, and *in view of his* faith."[34]

While the Missouri Synod thoroughly disavowed the accusation of false doctrine that Schmidt brought against Walther, a sizable portion of the Norwegian Synod supported Schmidt's position. For all practical purposes, the election controversy was over in the Missouri Synod in 1881. But the worst was yet to come for the Norwegian Synod.

The leaders of the Norwegian Synod, President H. A. Preus, Rev. J. A. Otteson, and Rev. U. V. Koren, along with most of the synod's pastors, did not align themselves with Schmidt. But Schmidt was able to gather a number of Norwegian pastors into his camp. They became known as the Anti-Missourians.

The argument Schmidt used to entice his hearers went something like this: The synod's pastors, since they taught an election of *some* and yet refused to make faith the cause of the election, could therefore not really teach that God wants the salvation of *all*. So Schmidt even charged them with Calvinism and implied those who followed Walther were destroying the doctrine of universal grace.[35] Schmidt and his cohorts insisted the only explanation as to why *some* were elected even though God willed the salvation of *all* lay in an "election in view of faith." But, as the late Professor T. A. Aaberg surmised, "[Schmidt] would now, however, have to explain how it came about that faith, being wholly and entirely the work of God, was not worked in the hearts of all who heard the Gospel, since God willed the salvation of all men."[36]

The controversy became so heated in the Norwegian Synod that on Good Friday 1883 President H. A. Preus, a formidable opponent of Schmidt, was carried physically out of his own church at Norway Grove (near DeForest, Wisconsin) by members who expressed loyalty to Schmidt. (This writer's grandfather had to witness that despicable event as a nine-year-old.)

In 1884 Rev. U. V. Koren produced an important essay entitled *En Redegjoerelse* ("An Accounting"), which upheld the scriptural teaching of election and refuted the synergism held by Schmidt and his followers. In this document Koren wrote:

> Since everything good in man is God's free and undeserved gift of grace, there is nothing in man which could induce God to elect him. Man's faith could not induce God to do this either, for faith is itself a free gift of grace from God,

which He has not been induced to give to man by anything
good in him, but alone by His mercy for Christ's sake;
"because God in His counsel, before the time of the world,
decided and ordained that He Himself, by the power of His
Holy Ghost, would produce and work in us, through the
Word, everything that pertains to our conversion."[37]

Many pastors from the Norwegian Synod signed the
document, but none of the Anti-Missourians did. So when
the Norwegian Synod met in convention at Stoughton,
Wisconsin, in 1887, the Anti-Missourians—about one-
third of the pastors, congregations, and members—left the
Norwegian Synod. This group joined with two other
Lutheran bodies that opposed the Norwegian Synod and
formed what became known as the United Church (Norwegian), a predecessor synod of today's Evangelical
Lutheran Church in America (ELCA).

Recalling this turbulent period of history, President
Wilhelm Petersen of Bethany Lutheran Seminary
remarked in his essay observing the 75th anniversary of
the Evangelical Lutheran Synod:

> Now the Norwegian Synod was left with but a minority of
> the Norwegian Lutherans in America, but it had saved the
> Gospel of salvation by grace alone, and on our 75th
> anniversary observance we thank God for this heritage.
> The whole controversy can be summed up as follows:
> Schmidt tried to explain the mystery why one is saved and
> the other lost, though God desires the salvation of all with
> equal earnestness. He attempted to solve that mystery by
> claiming that some men manifested a better conduct over
> towards grace than others in that they ceased to offer will-
> ful resistance to it. . . . The Synod, on the other hand,
> rejected both the synergistic and Calvinistic answers to
> the question why one is saved and the other lost. The
> Synod simply said with the Bible, that a man's salvation is

to be ascribed to God alone, that man has no power at any
time to choose salvation, but it is God who chooses. A
man's condemnation is the fault of man alone and that
God in no way is to be blamed, since he with equal
earnestness desires the salvation of all.[38]

Schmidt's error resurfaces

The election controversy among the Norwegian Lutherans did not end with the removal of the dissenters in the
late 1880s. Unfortunately the error of Schmidt surfaced
again for the Norwegian Synod about a decade later, when
a new president of the synod, Rev. H. G. Stub, came to
office in 1910.

From the time his presidency began, Stub promoted doctrinal discussions with the Hauge Synod[39] and the United
Church in an attempt to restore unity among Norwegian
Lutherans in America. Part of the reason for the push to
merge was the fact that all three synods were cooperating
on a new hymnbook (*The Lutheran Hymnary* of 1913). As a
result of the discussions, a document known as *Opgjør*
("Settlement") came into existence. Although many pastors and lay people of the Norwegian Synod objected to
what they correctly perceived was a compromise on the
doctrine of election, Stub defended and promoted it. A
minority group quickly formed and issued reports against
the acceptance of *Opgjør*, but unfortunately—after consid-
erable efforts—most of those who were on the side of the
minority joined the majority in going into the merger of
1917 with no substantial change in the document.

What was it about *Opgjør* that the minority at first
could not stomach? Aaberg explains:

> The Joint Committee [of the merging synods] declared in
> paragraph four: "We have agreed to reject all errors which

seek to explain away the mystery of election . . . either in a synergistic or a Calvinizing manner . . . every doctrine which . . . would deprive God of his glory as only Savior or . . . weaken man's sense of responsibility in relation to the acceptance or rejection of grace."[40]

Aaberg then goes on to say:

This paragraph ascribes to natural man a sense or feeling of responsibility regarding the acceptance of grace. Natural man, however, is "dead in trespasses and sins" (Eph. 2:1). Scripture says: "Ye must be born again" (John 3:7), and ascribes this work to the Holy Spirit working through the Gospel.[41]

In essence, the Third Article of the Apostles' Creed was at stake. For we find in Luther's explanation a rejection of a person's natural abilities and a complete dependence upon the Holy Spirit: "I believe that I cannot by my own thinking or choosing believe in Jesus Christ, my Lord, or come to him; but the Holy Spirit has called me by the gospel, enlightened me with his gifts, sanctified and kept me in the true faith."

On June 14, 1918, 13 pastors (including this writer's grandfather) and a number of lay people who could not in good conscience join the merger, held the founding meeting of a new synod at Lime Creek Lutheran Church in northern Iowa. Since it was wartime, the governor of Iowa had outlawed the use of foreign languages at public meetings. So this small group of Norwegians held their service in a cornfield just over the Minnesota state line— a mile or so from the Lime Creek church. President Bjug Harstad spoke fitting words to the assembly, based on Jeremiah 6:16, "This is what the LORD says: 'Stand at the crossroads and look; ask for the ancient paths, ask where the good way is, and walk in it, and you will find rest for your souls." This was the start of what today is known as the Evangelical Lutheran Synod (ELS), a long-time doctrinal partner of the Wisconsin Evangelical Lutheran Synod (WELS).

Who would have guessed that a controversy whose roots could be traced back to the days of Augustine and Melanchthon could have wreaked such havoc among so many Lutherans as late as 1917? In retrospect, the "in view of faith" expression used by Gerhard in the 1600s was inappropriate, no matter how much of an orthodox spin was assigned to it. Look at the misunderstanding it created some two hundred years later!

History's lesson for today's Lutherans

We can learn an important lesson from the election controversy in the Norwegian Synod. The fight for preserving the truth cannot hinge on the personalities of our leaders, but must be anchored in a clear and solid exposition of Scripture. Had Koren and Walther still been alive at the time the merger of the Norwegian Lutherans went into effect, the probability of the old conservative Norwegian Synod succumbing to a compromise on election in the early 1900s would have been slim. But who the leaders are should not overshadow the importance of preserving the doctrine itself. Scripture alone is to determine our stand, even when respected leaders pass from the scene. God's truth must not be forsaken! It is the only lamp for our feet and light for our path (Psalm 119:105).

The "in view of faith" expression does not belong in any description of God's foreknowledge and predestination of our souls. If it were actually the case that God chooses us because he foresaw we would be more apt to believe the gospel than others, the whole concept of grace would be thrown out.

God in his grace chooses people for salvation, and this salvation is realized for the individual person only through faith in the Redeemer. When people are lost in unbelief, it is the fault of sinners alone and never that of the all-gracious God, who wants all to be saved. "Between these two statements there is a great gulf fixed by Scripture itself, which it is vain presumption for mere man to seek to bridge by any sort of logical explanations or conclusions of his own."[42]

Election and The Lutheran Church—Missouri Synod

The Lutheran Church—Missouri Synod (LCMS) did not have trouble with election. However, in the 1930s the LCMS entered into doctrinal discussions with the American Lutheran Church (ALC), which had come into being in 1930 when the Iowa, Ohio, and Buffalo Synods merged. During these discussions, Missouri's view of church fellowship began to change. This brought about dissension between church bodies of the Synodical Conference and led to its dissolution in 1967.

One of the doctrines WELS and the ELS felt was inadequately addressed in the documents shared between the LCMS and the ALC was election. Too little was said about the points of doctrine and practice where there long had been disagreement. The "Common Confession" was adopted by the LCMS and the ALC in 1950, but this statement did not meet the approval of WELS and the ELS.

WELS and the ELS contended the "Common Confession" had to be rejected because it did not include some indispensable statements for defining the scriptural doctrine of election. In 1954 the WELS Conference of Presidents wrote: "Specifically, it lacks 'a clear and unmistakable statement that this election is an election *unto* faith; the positive assurance that this election is a *cause* of our salvation and what pertains thereto: definite recognition of the *certainty* of this election.'"[43]

The Synodical Conference partners asked the LCMS not to use the "Common Confession" for the purpose of effecting union with the ALC. However, this became a moot issue. By this time the LCMS already had broken off fellowship discussions with the ALC based on the "Common Confession" because of the ALC's intention to merge with the synods of the American Lutheran Conference (a more liberal alignment of church bodies). Even though the LCMS no longer defended the "Common Confession," the rift between the LCMS and the other synods in the Synodical Conference became irreparably impaired, particularly over the issue of church and prayer fellowship. The LCMS was on the verge of joining the National Lutheran Council (the forerunner of the Lutheran Council-USA [LCUSA]).

Once again, the dedication of leaders to stand only on Scripture in resolving a conflict over election and other doctrinal issues was praiseworthy! They understood that if one capitulates on election, a doctrine so intricately interwoven with God's saving grace, other teachings from the Bible also would fall by the wayside. The current liberalism prevailing in the ELCA today bears witness to this irrefutable fact.

The writer of the book of Hebrews tells us, "Remember your leaders"—but may we never forget the way he characterizes the leaders who really count—"who spoke the word of God to you" (13:7).

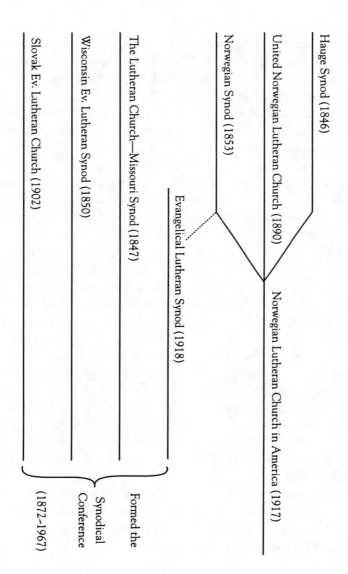

**Various Lutheran Synods Involved
in the Election Controversy during the Early 1900s**

9

Our Election Applied to Life

In his final speech to the people of Israel before his death, Moses included a powerful admonition. The people were to adhere closely to the words God had given them through Moses as they followed their new leader, Joshua, into the land of Canaan. "Take to heart all the words I have solemnly declared to you this day, so that you may command your children to obey carefully all the words of this law. They are not just idle words for you—they are your life" (Deuteronomy 32:46,47).

Not only would God's Word sustain and preserve his people as they were about to cross the Jordan River and live in the new land, this Word also would continue to be the full source of *life* for them through their earthly sojourn to the greater eternal Promised Land. Why did Moses call the words from God their "life"? He did so for one particular reason. At the heart and center of Moses' instruction and at the heart and center of all Scripture is the Rock of our salvation (Deuteronomy 32:4), the Rock of Ages—Christ Jesus!

Paraphrasing Moses we could also say, "The doctrine of election does not involve idle words, words for theologians to engage in their theoretical disputes. Rather, this doctrine has to do with one's *life*, for it consistently draws a person to Christ's cross and his grace for eternal hope." We are not implying here that a person has to understand election before he or she has eternal life. Faith in Christ's merits alone brings eternal life.

Many Christians remain ignorant about election—such as young children who are still growing in their Bible knowledge but are secure in their baptisms or spiritually young adults who have learned the nourishing milk of John 3:16 but are not yet ready for a solid food diet. The writer of Hebrews tells us, "Solid food is for the mature, who by constant use have trained themselves to distinguish good from evil" (5:14). Just as God gives us a wide variety of foods to build up our bodies, so he provides a variety of teachings in his Word that highlight the gospel to strengthen our souls. Election is one of these. It is intended for the comfort and edification of the soul that knows it has been purchased from sin and death by the holy blood of Christ.

When the apostle Paul reminded the Christians at Thessalonica that they had been chosen by God "from the beginning" (2 Thessalonians 2:13), he let them know that the teaching of election was to serve them for a superior cause. "He called you to this," says Paul, "through our gospel, that you might share in the glory of our Lord Jesus Christ" (verse 14). Our election to heaven from eternity is to remind our consciences repeatedly that we are victorious citizens of Christ destined for a better world. "Our citizenship is in heaven. And we eagerly await a Savior from there, the Lord Jesus Christ, who, by the power that enables him to bring everything under his control, will transform our lowly bodies so that they will be like his glorious body" (Philippians 3:20,21).

Our comfort in times of trial

The Scriptures lay out a panorama before our eyes that depicts the Savior's vital role for our lives. He is portrayed as the King (Zechariah 9:9), the Lamb of God (John 1:29), the Bread of Life (6:35), the Light of the World (8:12), the Gate (10:7), the True Vine (15:1), the Great High Priest (Hebrews 4:14), and the First and the Last (Revelation 1:17), to name just some of the descriptive titles. One of the most striking and beloved pictures is Jesus' description of himself as the Good Shepherd in John 10.

Although we discussed in a previous chapter how election gives us assurance, the comforting imagery of the Good Shepherd in John 10 is worthy of special attention in light of election. When Jesus speaks of his sheep being so firmly in the hands of his Father that no one—not even Satan—can snatch them away, he is drawing our thoughts to election. Because we have been *chosen* by God—a fact realized by faith in the Good Shepherd—we can always trust he is watching over us, protecting our faith for the time he brings us to heaven.

Listen to our Lord's familiar words: "My sheep listen to my voice; I know them, and they follow me. I give them eternal life, and they shall never perish; no one can snatch them out of my hand. My Father, who has given them to me, is greater than all; no one can snatch them out of my Father's hand. I and the Father are one" (verses 27-30).

The personal application here is this: Even though I sin daily and walk through the valley of the shadow of death, my Good Shepherd has picked me to be in his flock for time and eternity. And if he is truly one with the Father, as his name Immanuel (God with us) testifies, how can I ever doubt my safety? Christ himself has laid down his life for the sheep (verse 11). He has brought me and the rest of his sheep into his fold away from the wolves by his Spirit's regenerating power in Baptism. What's more, Christ even tells me his heavenly Father has chosen me. I have been elected to share in the glory of Christ forever!

The great comfort and security we have comes out even stronger in the original Greek. The actual translation is, "No one will snatch them" (verse 28). This says more than "no one can snatch them" (NIV). None of the Lord's elect will ever be lost! They will have a place in the eternal rest! As we think of the way the Good Shepherd cradles us in his bosom—by means of his Word and sacraments—we live each day with this steadfast assurance: Nothing at all can ever separate us from being with our Lord (Romans 8:38,39).

Do we question whether we are among the elect when troubles descend on our homes and families or when we find ourselves in the fires of affliction? Are there moments when we feel like Job, who said: "Your hands shaped me and made me. Will you now turn and destroy me? Remember that you molded me like clay. Will you now turn me to dust again?" (Job 10:8,9).

A Christian farmer had such questions. He too had learned that he was chosen by God. But then calamity struck. Right before the busy harvest season, the farmer had to enter the hospital for emergency surgery on his heart. The doctors told him his chances of survival were not very good. As they were preparing him for surgery, the Christian farmer told his wife he was afraid he would die in the hospital. The operation was successful, and the man was out of the hospital within ten days. When he arrived home, though, he did some more worrying. He worried that his crops were going to be ruined because he wouldn't be able to do his own harvesting. His God-fearing wife made him think of what he so quickly seemed to forget: "Honey," she said, "God took care of your big worry in restoring your life. Don't you think he can be trusted to take care of the crops?"

Penetrating words! They apply to us all in a far deeper way. Steeped in sin from conception and birth— evidenced by our actual sins of thought, word, and deed— we humans faced life's greatest problem: We were like wandering sheep at the edge of a cliff ready to fall into an abyss. The abyss we were headed for was hell itself. For we read, "Cursed is everyone who does not continue to do everything written in the Book of the Law" (Galatians 3:10). But God snatched us from the edge. Our Shepherd's mighty arms kept us from eternal ruin! While we were spiritually dead, God brought us new life. He put us on the pathway to life eternal. How? Only through faith in Christ's atoning death and resurrection. By faith we exclaim, "While we were still sinners, Christ died for us" (Romans 5:8). So loving is our God that he would have us who trust in his grace hear again and again how firmly he has made us his own. In effect, he says to all who believe in his name: "Rest assured. I have called you to be mine. I have chosen you from eternity. I, as the Good Shepherd, have drawn your soul to my side in Holy Baptism."

Parroting the advice of that farmer's faithful wife, we can reflect on our election and now say: "Why worry, O my soul? God has taken care of my biggest trouble. He has delivered me from the worst death. He tells me I was chosen by mercy to be his own long before I was born. So solidly has he cemented me in his camp!" Remember how it was in the context of discussing our election that the apostle Paul remarked, "If God is for us, who can be against us?" (Romans 8:31). God spared *our* lives by not sparing his very own Son! And since he now calls his believers "chosen," dare any of us question his promise that he will handle for our benefit every one of life's cares that comes our way?

Not for promoting carnal security

The comfort of election applies to those who know they have been saved by Christ and thus thankfully desire to live each day "no longer . . . for themselves but for him who died for them and was raised again" (2 Corinthians 5:15). It is a violation of God's Word to take any doctrine that lends comfort to the sinner and twist it into a license to do evil. Since the Christian is both saint and sinner at the same time until departing this life, a daily battle must be waged against the insidious notion that one's election assurance means there isn't as great of a need to live a sanctified life. If one were to boast, "I'm saved by Christ, so how I live under the commandments isn't important," this would contradict Paul's words in Romans 6:1-4. There he states:

What shall we say, then? Shall we go on sinning so that grace may increase? By no means! We died to sin; how can we live in it any longer? Or don't you know that all of us who were baptized into Christ Jesus were baptized into his death? We were therefore buried with him through baptism into death in order that, just as Christ was raised from the dead through the glory of the Father, we too may · live a new life.

In his book *The Christian Faith*, Dr. Robert Kolb writes:

> The doctrine of election dare not be discussed with someone who is claiming that the grace it offers permits the elect to sin. . . . When someone asks, "Am I among the elect?" Christians respond, "Why do you want to know?" Those who wish to use the doctrine of election as an excuse or license for sin will not understand what it means to be God's chosen child. Such people need to hear God's Law as it crushes their sinful pretension.[44]

On the other hand, for those who see their sinfulness for what it is and eagerly hold to the Savior's cross, Kolb quickly adds: "Those who fear they have so offended God that they can never be or become his children are crying out for God's assurance that he has chosen them to be his own."[45]

For any individual person who is confident of heaven for a carnal reason—one that appeals to the sinful flesh, such as basing one's hope on an outward connection with the church—a stark warning must be issued. The true security offered in election can only be found *in Christ*. Earthly connections will not do. We need the real holiness that saves: the holiness from the cross. The holiness of Christ covering our sins is found in the gospel. Hold to the gospel! There is true security. All else fails. There is *no other way* to be among the elect people of God.

A man who grew up in a good Christian home once told me: "I don't think it is so necessary for me to go to church. Oh, Pastor, don't get me wrong. I believe, and I know I'll go to heaven. I was taught all the stories about Jesus when I was a little boy. But I don't see any great value in hearing the same thing over and over again." He obviously had not grasped the gist of the Third Commandment, nor had he pondered the words of Hebrews, "Let us not give up meeting together, as some are in the habit of doing" (10:25). But what is worse, this man failed to see the necessary distinction between the two great doctrines of law and gospel. He *claimed* to know the gospel, and if he had been asked, I'm sure he would have *claimed* to be of the elect. Yet, he did not perceive that the gospel, as well as election, can only be applied when the law has already done its work in convicting the heart of sin and the desperate need for the Savior. In addition, his carnally secure heart would have to hear this sharp rebuke from God's law: "If you think you are standing firm, be careful that you don't fall!" (1 Corinthians 10:12).

Driven to the well of living water

We who look in the mirror of God's law and realize our wretchedness but then hear from the gospel how Christ has put away our shame learn from election *where* to quench our thirsty souls. Election drives us to drink freely of the water of life offered by the Lord Jesus. "Whoever is thirsty, let him come; and whoever wishes, let him take the free gift of the water of life" (Revelation 22:17). Because our election is always based on the Word, we flee for refuge to the infinite mercy of Christ flowing as streams of living water in the written, spoken, and sacramental Word of God.

From God's standpoint, our election is always sure. The only way election remains a certainty with each Christian is by drinking from the source of unchanging truth: God's Word. Election is never meant to stagnate our souls, but to revitalize them. As we live our lives centered around the Word of God, that life-giving Word spews forth to our thirsty souls the full assurance that Christ is our personal Savior from sin, death, Satan, and hell. How can heaven ever be denied us, as long as we are *in Christ?*

Application in confirmation

Election may receive little attention in catechism classes. Usually only one or two questions specifically cover election in the different instruction books used with our youth.

However, when we discuss with our children in our homes the Third Article of the Apostles' Creed, we have a natural opportunity to speak to them about their own personal election. Great care needs to be taken in presenting this doctrine. It is to be taught only as pure gospel, for it finds its application to the student's soul only in connection with Christ's grace and the means the Holy Spirit uses to work and preserve faith.

> If we continue to proclaim the *sola gratia* [grace alone] firmly in connection with the doctrines of man's depravity, objective justification, and conversion, we have gone a long way in warding off synergistic thoughts in the doctrine of election, which besides bringing the comfort this doctrine gives, is the chief aim of our teaching it, for he who trusts in himself loses his Lord.[46]

Opposing modern-day synergism

Another important use of the crucial election doctrine is to refute the common error of intermingling God's grace with our effort at receiving the gospel. *Decision theology* is a term used to describe the view of many Reformed theologians today who insist believers at least in some small way yield up their will to God (synergism) so that they consciously *decide* to repent of sin and follow Christ. Many televangelists, including the crusade specialist Rev. Billy Graham, are promoters of decision theology, which is just a return to the age-old error of synergism.

Although "grace" rolls off the lips of the preachers who espouse decision theology, some trademark expressions betray their real understanding of grace: "Won't you decide tonight to come down in front and give your heart to the Lord Jesus Christ?" "Invite Christ to come into your life." "Won't you sincerely invite the Lord Jesus into your heart and surrender your will completely to him right now?" "Give your life to Christ." "Inviting Christ into your life is absolutely the most important decision you will ever make!" And a very common expression used almost universally, even in reference to salvation, is the hackneyed phrase "God helps those who help themselves." Someone has said that a heavy dose of "I" runs through each encounter with Jesus when many of the "electronic church" ascend the pulpit or take the stage.

Graham, in his book *How to Be Born Again*, says, "The context of John 3 teaches that the new birth is something that God does for man when man is willing to yield to God."[47] Again, he writes, "Any person who is willing to trust Jesus Christ as his personal Savior and Lord can receive the new birth now."[48] Statements like these deny that people by nature are totally spiritually dead in transgressions and sins (Ephesians 2:1).

Our election stands as a testimony to the truth that God has "called us to a holy life—not because of anything we have done but because of his own purpose and grace. This grace was given us in Christ Jesus before the beginning of time" (2 Timothy 1:9). The predestination of our souls, the planning of our coming into contact with the means of grace, the preservation of our souls while "treading the verge of Jordan" until landing "safe on Canaan's side" (CW 331:3), is entirely the work of God (1 Corinthians 12:3). If it were not, we would receive no genuine comfort. Just as it was for Luther before the Reformation, so all people would be forced to ask, "How can I ever know if I have done *my part* to get the saving 'grace'?"

Thankfully, we teach an election that is completely by grace in every way. With the writers of the Formula of Concord, we concur, "It [this election teaching] is indeed a useful, salutary, and comforting doctrine, for it mightily substantiates the article that we are justified and saved without our works and merit, purely by grace and solely for Christ's sake."[49] Let's use election to combat any overt or camouflaged attempt by modern-day preachers to have us raise the old banner of synergism.

Decision theology is not the only spiritual poison to be warded off with the antidote of the correct doctrine of election. The teaching of universalism is sweeping across various denominations. This false doctrine gives an easy answer to the dilemma "Why are some saved and not others?" It asserts no one ultimately will be lost to damnation or—if some are—it will only be the hardened capital criminals.

Again, the election doctrine destroys such thinking. Christ is clearly presented as the only way to be sure of one's inclusion in the elect. "Salvation is found in no one else, for there is no other name under heaven given to men by which we must be saved" (Acts 4:12). Either people believe in Christ the Savior and will enjoy everlasting life in heaven, or else they do not believe and therefore will be destroyed eternally, body and soul in hell.

How election affects all doctrine

"Unsoundness in this doctrine," writes Rev. Otto Eckert, "works like a vicious leaven and leads to loose thinking, indifference toward other doctrines, lack of doctrinal discipline, lax practice, and unionism. It is a first step on the road to liberalism; therefore the public doctrine of any church body must sound a clear note both thetically and antithetically in this doctrine."[50]

We cannot help referring back for a moment to the election controversy in the old Norwegian Synod. The difference on election may have seemed like a minor matter to many. But a church body that tolerates error on such an important doctrine as election, a doctrine closely related to the proper teaching on original sin and justification by grace, is headed only for further departures from the Word. One bad apple in the bushel basket in time corrupts all the others. Such a sizable apple as election, if permitted a bruising and bashing, will not fail to spread decay quickly to the others. Look at where the old Norwegian Synod, a bastion of doctrinal conservatism in the early 1900s, is today. Merger after merger after merger has allowed compromise on all sorts of doctrines, even to the point where the present ELCA (the synod where most of the Norwegian Lutherans have now landed) refuses to use the word *inerrant* to characterize the words of Holy Scripture.

May we pray that God would preserve us from tainting his teaching of election, as well as any of his other doctrines!

Election's bearing on mission work

Imagine how uneasy a car salesman would feel if the owner of his national corporation sent him a personal memo saying: "Try to sell to everyone. But I want you to know personally that while you are giving your sales pitch, it is not going to be effective. Why? I have already determined the proper buyers and also those whom I forbid to own one of our cars." Suppose in front of his showcase window the salesman had a huge billboard that read, "These cars are meant for everyone." Do you think he would believe it himself? Do you think he would try very hard to persuade prospective buyers? Would he maybe have a careless approach to his selling? "What's the use in making a sales pitch," he might say, "if the head of the company has predetermined every buyer and everyone forbidden to buy?"

Some people think this kind of illustration (which is faulty as a comparison with election) exposes the concept of mission work as superfluous. They know God has said, "Go and make disciples of all nations" (Matthew 28:19), but they cynically suspect God doesn't want everyone to believe. In fact, they believe he has foreordained many to refuse the message of Christ and perish in hell. We should not be surprised if some in the Reformed camp were to experience such thoughts in respect to mission work. The Calvinistic system of election easily lends itself to a warped view of spreading the gospel.

But when election is correctly taught, mission work deserves and receives supreme attention. A quick review of what Scripture teaches impresses on us the urgency of spreading the Word:

- God from eternity has chosen people to believe in Christ and have eternal life.

- This choosing is realized here in time only by faith in Christ's free forgiveness of sins.

- Christ has redeemed the world and offers forgiveness in the gospel as a gift meant for everyone.

- God truly wants all to believe and be saved.

- Faith is worked only through the Word and sacraments.

- The Holy Spirit uses the Word to turn sinners' hearts to Christ. Those who reject the message are lost by their own fault.

When God sends his called public servants to preach and teach the gospel and when he motivates all Christians to share Christ as members of the universal priesthood of all believers, he is not insincere about reaching lost souls. Since he has atoned for the sins of all with the blood of his Son (1 John 2:2), the Word he now wants proclaimed is far from being an empty shell. The Almighty himself has invested real power in it. It is so much "the power of God" (Romans 1:16), that the apostle Paul told the Corinthians, "By this gospel you are saved, if you hold firmly to the word I preached to you" (1 Corinthians 15:2). No less import was given to the Word when Paul spoke to the Thessalonians: "When you received the word of God . . . you accepted it not as the word of men, but as it actually is, the word of God, which is at work [the Greek word is related to the English word *energize*] in you who believe" (1 Thessalonians 2:13).

Quite opposite from the auto executive in the illustration above, God so much "wants all men to be saved" (1 Timothy 2:4), that he makes salvation a free gift from start to finish. He entertains no thoughts of people "buying" it with any merit. In fact, if the righteousness of Christ had to be earned by sinners even to the slightest degree, it would be a righteousness based on the law and not the gospel. But Scripture assures us: "A man is not justified by observing the law, but by faith in Jesus Christ" (Galatians 2:16). "For we maintain that a man is justified by faith apart from observing the law" (Romans 3:28). So the very nature of the gospel conveys the earnestness of God in desiring every sinner with no exception to have forgiveness and also everlasting life.

A key Bible verse in discussing election and mission work is Isaiah 55:10,11. Speaking through his prophet, God says:

> As the rain and the snow come down from heaven, and do not return to it without watering the earth and making it bud and flourish, so that it yields seed for the sower and bread for the eater, so is my word that goes out from my mouth: It will not return to me empty [the Hebrew word literally means "in vain" or "without effect"], but will accomplish what I desire and achieve the purpose for which I sent it.

Precisely because we know God uses his Word to work faith in Christ's universal redemption, we go about mission work with great zeal and joy. We who bring the message to others cannot tell exactly who the chosen or elect are. Nor should we try to ascertain this. If Christian missionaries were aware beforehand of who would believe and retain the faith to the end, they would not speak the Word universally, as the Lord has commanded us (Mark 16:15).

Without trying to peer beyond what God has revealed to us concerning election, we go about mission work happily leaving all things to God's direction. As the Word is taught, it is he and he alone who works the results where and when he pleases. Jesus was referring to this when he told Nicodemus: "The wind blows wherever it pleases. You hear its sound, but you cannot tell where it comes from or where it is going. So it is with everyone born of the Spirit" (John 3:8). We are the poor servants of God carrying the precious Word: jars of clay (2 Corinthians 4:7) containing living water to be poured out on the parched soil of thirsty souls. But God himself causes the plant of faith to grow. "Neither he who plants nor he who waters is anything," said the great missionary Paul, "but only God, who makes things grow" (1 Corinthians 3:7).

While preaching in Pisidian Antioch, Paul and Barnabas experienced a mixed reaction to their preaching. The Jews talked abusively against them, but many Gentiles believed. Note how carefully Luke records the converts: "All who were appointed for eternal life believed" (Acts 13:48). By our gospel efforts we pray that God will bring the elect into his kingdom. We sing in our mission hymn "Rise, O Light of Gentile Nations":

> Savior, shine in all your glory
> On the nations near and far;
> From the highways and the byways
> Call them forth, O Morning Star.
> Guide them whom your grace has chosen
> Out of Satan's dreadful thrall
> To the mansions of your Father—
> There is room for sinners all. (CW 577:4)

Our view of election definitely colors our perspective on mission work. Are we convinced that God alone elects and calls people through the Word and sacraments? Are we convinced that people who do not hear the Word in their lifetimes are lost eternally? If a person does not come into contact with God's Word, we are bound to conclude this individual has not been connected by faith to the benefits of Christ's cross. The popular author Josh McDowell, in his book *Answers to Tough Questions*, disagrees. He contends, "No one will be condemned for not ever hearing of Jesus Christ."[51] But Scripture answers: "How can they [the heathen] believe in the one of whom they have not heard? And how can they hear without someone preaching to them? Consequently, faith comes from hearing the message, and the message is heard through the word of Christ" (Romans 10:14,17). No wonder Christians down through the ages have been known to give witnessing for Christ top billing!

"Special people do special work." That is a fitting expression for Christians when the word *special* is carefully defined. What makes us special? It isn't that we are better by nature than others. It isn't that we have more things to offer God by nature than others. We are special because of Jesus Christ, the Cornerstone on which we rest. By faith in him, our heavenly Father tells us we are chosen people. "You are a chosen people, a royal priesthood, a holy nation, a people belonging to God" (1 Peter 2:9). Christians also have very special work to do. It is a natural response to our being God's special or chosen people. God says to us, "You are a chosen people . . . that you may declare the praises of him who called you out of darkness into his wonderful light" (verse 9).

A large promotion was once given to an officer in a business. Along with it went a number of fancy titles and awards. Something strange happened, though. After receiving all those, the man gradually became preoccupied with the special treatment he was getting and neglected the very work he had been promoted to do. The business began to suffer. He would just sit in his office and stare at the exclusive nameplates on his desk and the gold-trimmed plaque on the wall. But what good did it do this man to be called special if he didn't care at all about doing the work he had been asked to do?

Fellow believers, we have received a special title: *chosen!* We bear this title because of the hard labor of another—the One who trudged along the dusty road to Calvary. We are moved out of love and thankfulness even more diligently to be about the Father's business, the life-saving work we have been called to do. "We cannot help speaking about what we have seen and heard" (Acts 4:20).

Endnotes

[1]Martin Luther, *What Luther Says: An Anthology*, compiled by Ewald M. Plass, 3 vols. (St. Louis: Concordia Publishing House, 1959), p. 1160.

[2]Siegbert Becker, *The Word Goes On: Sermons* (Milwaukee: Northwestern Publishing House, 1972), p. 70.

[3]Joh. P. Meyer, "The Holy Spirit Creator," *Northwestern Lutheran*, Vol. 39, No. 21 (October 19, 1952), p. 325.

[4]Formula of Concord, Solid Declaration, Article XI:45, *The Book of Concord: The Confessions of the Evangelical Lutheran Church*, translated and edited by Theodore G. Tappert (Philadelphia: Fortress Press, 1959), p. 624. Besides this article in the Formula of Concord, no extensive treatment of election is found in *The Book of Concord*.

[5]Irwin J. Habeck, *Ephesians* (Milwaukee: Northwestern Publishing House, 1985), pp. 18,19.

[6]Formula of Concord, Epitome, Article II:12,13, Tappert, pp. 522,523.

[7]Large Catechism, Part II:38, Tappert, p. 411.

[8]*Lutheran Sentinel*, Vol. 72, No. 2 (February 1989), p. 10.

[9]Quoted in Wilbert Kreiss, "The Lutheran Theology of Certitude," *The Lutheran Synod Quarterly*, Vol. XX, No. 1 (March 1980), p. 58.

[10]Smalcald Articles, Part III, Article VIII:10, Tappert p. 313.

[11]Formula of Concord, Solid Declaration, Article XI:87,88, Tappert, p. 631.

[12]George Stoeckhardt, *The Epistle to the Romans*, translated by Erwin Koehlinger (St. Louis: Concordia Seminary, 1943), p. 116 (emphasis added).

[13]Stoeckhardt, *The Epistle to the Romans*, p. 116.

[14]Paul E. Kretzmann, *Popular Commentary of the Bible*, New Testament, Vol. 2 (St. Louis: Concordia Publishing House, 1923), p. 47.

[15]Edward W. A. Koehler, *A Summary of Christian Doctrine* (St. Louis: Concordia Publishing House, 1939), p. 170.

[16]Formula of Concord, Solid Declaration, Article XI:34, Tappert, p. 622.

[17]Smalcald Articles, Part III, Article II:4, Tappert, p. 303.

[18]Formula of Concord, Solid Declaration, Article I:8, Tappert, p. 510.

[19]Formula of Concord, Epitome, Article I:15, Tappert, p. 468.

[20]Formula of Concord, Solid Declaration, Article XI:55, Tappert, p. 625.

[21]Lutherans using the New International Version (NIV) may be troubled by an unfortunate translation of Romans 9:22. The NIV reads, "What if God, choosing to show his wrath and make his power known, bore with great patience the objects of his wrath—prepared for destruction?" Prof. John Jeske, an original participant in the NIV project, warns: "The casual reader of Romans 9:22f. in the NIV is likely to assume that the two phrases 'prepared for destruction' and 'prepared in advance for glory' [in verse 23] are parallel in the original, that the same Greek verbs are used to describe the two groups of people. The text, however, does not say that God prepared

certain people for destruction; as a result of their unbelief they were ripe for destruction. The translation is not a good one" (*Wisconsin Lutheran Quarterly*, Vol. 85, No. 2, p. 107).

[22]Philip Schaff, editor, *The Creeds of Christendom*, Vol. 3 (Grand Rapids: Baker Book House, 1985), pp. 608,609.

[23]Schaff, *The Creeds of Christendom*, Vol. 3, p. 610.

[24]Philip Melanchthon, *Loci Communes*, translated by J. A. O. Preus (St. Louis: Concordia Publishing House, 1992), p. 44.

[25]On this, read Franz Pieper's remarks in his *Christian Dogmatics*, Vol. 3 (St. Louis: Concordia Publishing House, 1953), p. 487.

[26]Quoted in Heinrich Schmid, *The Doctrinal Theology of the Lutheran Church* (Minneapolis: Augsburg Publishing House, 1961), p. 272.

[27]Joh. P. Meyer, "The Holy Spirit Creator," *Northwestern Lutheran*, Vol. 39, No. 20 (October 5, 1952), p. 311.

[28]Quoted in Sigurd C. Ylvisaker, *Grace for Grace* (Mankato, Minn.: Lutheran Synod Book Co., 1943), p. 183.

[29]Formula of Concord, Epitome, Article XI:20, Tappert, p. 497. Article XI is devoted entirely to election.

[30]Stoeckhardt, *The Epistle to the Romans*, p. 114.

[31]Quoted in Ylvisaker, *Grace for Grace*, p. 172.

[32]Theodore A. Aaberg, *A City Set On a Hill* (Mankato, Minn.: Board of Publications, Evangelical Lutheran Synod, 1968), p. 27 (emphasis original).

[33]C. F. W. Walther, *The Proper Distinction Between Law and Gospel* (St. Louis: Concordia Publishing House, 1928), pp. 272,273 (emphasis added).

[34]Walther, *The Proper Distinction Between Law and Gospel*, p. 3 (emphasis added).

[35]Aaberg, *A City Set On a Hill*, p. 27.

[36]Aaberg, *A City Set On a Hill*, p. 28.

[37]Quoted in Ylvisaker, *Grace for Grace*, pp. 184,185. Koren's quote is from Formula of Concord, Solid Declaration, Article XI:44, *Concordia Triglotta: The Symbolical Books of the Ev.*

Lutheran Church (St. Louis: Concordia Publishing House, 1921), p. 1077.

[38]*76th Report: Regular Convention of the Evangelical Lutheran Synod,* June 20–24, 1993, p. 95.

[39]The Hauge Synod was formed in 1876 as a splinter group of the Eielsen Synod. Like the Eielsen Synod, its members were primarily of Norwegian descent and promoted Lutheran Pietism, lay preaching, and the necessity of a conscious conversion experience.

[40]Aaberg, *A City Set On a Hill*, p. 50. Aaberg quotes Richard C. Wolf, *Documents of Lutheran Unity in America* (Philadelphia: Fortress Press:, 1966), p. 234.

[41]Aaberg, *A City Set On a Hill*, p. 50.

[42]Ylvisaker, *Grace for Grace*, p. 192.

[43]Quoted from the tract "Chosen By Grace From Eternity," issued by the WELS Conference of Presidents in 1954, p. 6.

[44]Robert Kolb, *The Christian Faith* (St. Louis: Concordia Publishing House, 1993), p. 175.

[45]Kolb, *The Christian Faith*, p. 175.

[46]Otto Eckert, "The Relation of Time to Eternity in God's Dealing with Man as Concerning the Doctrine of Election," *Our Great Heritage*, Vol. 3, edited by Lyle W. Lange (Milwaukee: Northwestern Publishing House, 1991), p. 75.

[47]Billy Graham, *How to Be Born Again* (Waco, Tex.: Word, 1977), p. 150.

[48]Graham, *How to Be Born Again*, p. 152.

[49]Formula of Concord, Solid Declaration, Article XI:43, Tappert, p. 623.

[50]Eckert, "The Relation of Time to Eternity," p. 76.

[51]Josh McDowell, *Answers to Tough Questions* (San Bernardino, Cal: Here's Life Publishers, Inc., 1980), p. 131.

For Further Reading

Aaberg, Theodore A. *A City Set On a Hill*. Mankato, Minn. Board of Publications, Evangelical Lutheran Synod, 1968.

Eckert, Otto. "The Relation of Time to Eternity in God's Dealing with Man as Concerning the Doctrine of Election," in *Our Great Heritage*, Vol. 3. Edited by Lyle W. Lange. Milwaukee: Northwestern Publishing House, 1991.

Kramer, Fred. "The Doctrine of Election, or Predestination" in *The Abiding Word*, Vol. 1. Edited by Theodore Laetsch. St. Louis: Concordia Publishing House, 1946.

Preus, Robert. "The Doctrine of Election as Taught by the Seventeenth Century Lutheran Dogmaticians" in *Our Great Heritage*, Vol. 3. Edited by Lyle W. Lange. Milwaukee: Northwestern Publishing House, 1991.

Formula of Concord, Article XI. *The Book of Concord: The Confessions of the Evangelical Lutheran Church*. Translated and edited by Theodore G. Tappert. Philadelphia: Fortress Press, 1959.

Stoeckhardt, George. *Predestination Election*. Translated by Erwin Koehlinger. Fort Wayne: Concordia Theological Seminary Press.

Scripture Index

1 Timothy
  1:19—75
  2:4—10,108

2 Timothy
  1:9—27,60,61,105
  3:16—69
  4:3—71

Titus
  2:14—29
  3:4,5—13
  3:5—36,59

Hebrews
  3:6—36
  4:14—97
  5:14—96
  6:4-6—75
  10:25—102
  10:26-29—75
  11:1—54
  13:7—93
  13:8—54

1 Peter
  1:3-5—57
  1:19—54
  1:20—27
  2:9—111

2 Peter
  1:10—56
  1:19—56
  2:1—75
  2:5—70
  3:9—10,61

1 John
  2:2—11,55,74,75,108
  3:20—62

Revelation
  1:17—97
  3:20—45,46
  13:8—27
  22:17—102

Subject Index